A must-read for all fans in Singapore and Malaysia and of football in general, John Duerden has been writing about Asian football for a long time and really captures the unique story of the game in that part of the world with an engaging, lively and well-written book.

Marcus Christenson,
football editor of *The Guardian*

All fans of Singapore and Malaysia football should read this great book that really tells the story of football and a unique rivalry.

Aleksandar Durić,
former Singapore national striker

Great job! The book is a wonderful insight into football in Singapore and Malaysia and brought back so many memories.

Daniel Bennett,
Singapore international

A really enjoyable read and a wonderful reminder of just how colourful football is in Singapore and Malaysia.

John Wilkinson,
former Singapore international

For football fans on both sides of the Causeway, there's only one match that really stirs local souls. Singapore against Malaysia, the Lions against the Tigers, neighbour against neighbour. It's always the big one, perhaps the only one.

Like England and Germany or Brazil and Argentina, the Causeway rivalry stretches back more than a century. All else can be lost, but Singapore and Malaysia cannot lose to each other.

John Duerden analyses this fascinating relationship, from the embryonic stages of the Malaysia Cup to the present day, a time when both nations find themselves struggling in the region.

Well researched and extremely informative, Duerden's insightful book pulls no punches in detailing the entrenched football failings in both countries, including the polarising foreign talent schemes, the lack of suitable playing facilities and the paucity of quality coaching.

But the book also explains why Causeway clashes are so special, why players, managers and fans look forward to these games more than any other. Indeed as both nations seek to navigate a way forward in the 21st century, it becomes clear that as long as the tribal flame still burns, the local game has a fighting chance of survival.

Ironically, the Lions and Tigers have never needed each other more than they do now. And that's why Duerden's book needs to be read now.

Neil Humphreys,
bestselling author of *Return to a Sexy Island,*
Match Fixer, Premier Leech and *Rich Kill Poor Kill*

JOHN DUERDEN

LIONS AND TIGERS

The story of football in
Singapore and Malaysia

Marshall Cavendish
Editions

Editor: She-reen Wong
Designer: Bernard Go Kwang Meng
All photos: Weixiang Lim, courtesy of *FourFourTwo*

Published by Marshall Cavendish Editions
An imprint of Marshall Cavendish International

A member of the
Times Publishing Group

Other Marshall Cavendish Offices:
Marshall Cavendish Corporation. 99 White Plains Road, Tarrytown NY 10591-9001, USA • Marshall Cavendish International (Thailand) Co Ltd. 253 Asoke, 12th Flr, Sukhumvit 21 Road, Klongtoey Nua, Wattana, Bangkok 10110, Thailand • Marshall Cavendish (Malaysia) Sdn Bhd, Times Subang, Lot 46, Subang Hi-Tech Industrial Park, Batu Tiga, 40000 Shah Alam, Selangor Darul Ehsan, Malaysia

Marshall Cavendish is a registered trademark of Times Publishing Limited

National Library Board, Singapore Cataloguing-in-Publication Data

Name(s): Duerden, John, 1972-
Title: Lions and tigers : the story of football in Singapore and Malaysia / John Duerden.
Other title(s): Story of football in Singapore and Malaysia
Description: Singapore : Marshall Cavendish Editions, an imprint of Marshall Cavendish International, [2017]
Identifier(s): OCN 996882814 | ISBN 978-981-47-7171-9 (paperback)
Subject(s): LCSH: Soccer--Singapore. | Soccer--Malaysia. | Soccer players--Singapore. | Soccer players--Malaysia. | Soccer matches.
Classification: DDC 796.3340959--dc23

Printed in Singapore by JCS Digital Solutions Pte Ltd

For my girls – Myung-joo, Danbi and Yubi

CONTENTS

Prologue   9

Introduction: The AFF Cup and the Puskas Award
               —Summing Up Football in Singapore and Malaysia   13

Chapter 1:   The Early Days: Singapore, Selangor, Penang   31
               and the Malaysia Cup

Chapter 2:   The Sixties, Seventies and the Singapore   46
               and Selangor series

Chapter 3:   Singapore versus the States: LionsXII in Malaysia   52

Chapter 4:   The Lions and Tigers in the 20th Century   63

Chapter 5:   21st Century International Meetings   81

Chapter 6:   The Stars: Fandi, SuperMokh and the Rest   103

Chapter 7:   Foreign Influence: Singaporean Style   126

Chapter 8:   Foreign Influence: The Malaysia Method   146

Chapter 9:   Federation Revolution?   166

Epilogue   180

PROLOGUE

In football Malaysia and Singapore shouldn't be different when you think about it—but they are.

—Radojko "Raddy" Avramović,
former Singapore national coach

The first time I crossed the Causeway was by bus. It was a trip from Melaka, after a lazy couple of days exploring one of the most historic cities in Asia. Jumping off at the Malaysian side of the border, I was assured that the driver would wait ("however long you take, or half an hour at least" came the answer with a smirk and glint in the eye—it was obviously not the first time he had been asked that question). But it is hard to resist the temptation to rush through, just to be sure. Being stranded on the Singaporean side of the border would be one of the less stressful places in the world to be stranded, and you are hardly 24 hours from civilisation. Still, it is a scenario best avoided.

Once the scramble was over, there was time to relax for the short drive to Bugis, not quite the gleaming vision of Singapore you expect from the brochures and later the iconic F1 race, but an interesting one nonetheless. Here was a teeming district full of bustling shops, supermarkets and subterranean shopping malls that felt very Asian and not much like the skyscrapers around the bay or the more sedate and genteel surroundings of Orchard Road.

Coming from the United Kingdom, the idea that you could just drive across the border to a different country was a novel and exciting concept. I had also spent lots of time living in South Korea, hanging off the far eastern side of the Eurasian landmass, like an upside-down rabbit, at least so the locals said.

But while the "Land of the Morning Calm"—a massive misnomer, at least in the manic capital of Seoul—is geographically part of the continent, practically, it is an island too. You can't drive anywhere else from South Korea. At least you can put your car on a ferry in England and emerge the other side in France, the Netherlands, Belgium, Sweden or Ireland and then drive merrily on your way, but it is not so easy in Korea.

For personal reasons, then, crossing a land border is an exciting thing to do; and crossing from Malaysia to Singapore doubly so, even though thousands who cross the Causeway every day to go to work see it as part of a dull commute.

As Avramović says, it should not be different, but it is. Sure, the laska varies, but then it is never the same in different parts of Malaysia. The satay is obviously more delicious in Malaysia, but then the curry *laksa* in Singapore can be divine; and one of the best things about the country was enjoying that dish (well, two as one was never quite enough) upstairs in Changi Terminal One, a canteen-style part of the airport that seems to have disappeared in the name of progress.

It is like the hawker centres. They should be the same but are different. In my experience, the ones in Singapore feel a little more solid and permanent than their Malaysian counterparts. But then, I much prefer to have my food brought to the table, as has always been the case for me in Malaysia and not Singapore. That enables one to try lots of different dishes and it is a real pleasure to walk past a stall, shout out a dish and a table number, and move on to the next one to try something else. It's much harder to do so if you have to physically wait while they cook and go get it yourself. Having food brought to your table also gives you time to relax, drink a cold beer and talk about what is really important—and in many cases, that is football.

The beautiful game is still important in this part of the world. There seem to be more Manchester United fans in Malaysia, with Liverpool the number one foreign team over the border. Domestically, Malaysians still seem to be in love with the game a little more than their Singaporean cousins, who need a little more encouragement to get their football juices flowing. Perhaps it is due to the fact that in a country like Malaysia with its regions, states and far-flung destinations, local pride comes into effect in a way that it is simply not feasible in a small city state such as Singapore.

There seems to be something in the statement made by the man known as "Raddy", who had spent a decade in charge of the Singapore national team and had plenty of chances to test his team against Malaysia and plenty of opportunities to watch the Malaysian league.

While it is impressive to see the loyalty given to English football teams, it is better still to talk of the local game and its rich history.

In modern times, there is plenty of talk about history. If you are in either country and the talk turns to the local football scene, then you can guarantee one thing: in the time it takes to fry a passable *char kway teow*, someone is going to start talking about the days gone by. As an Englishman, I have some sympathy with this habit and if—as they say—the past is a foreign country, it is also sweeter than a Mokhtar Dahari thunderbolt.

That is why now is the best time to write this book. There are plenty of issues and problems, and not that much optimism about, but there is still plenty to love about football in these two countries. They have a rich history, a fascinating present and a future full of possibilities.

While this is about Malaysia and Singapore football, their relationship, rivalry and history, I hope that it is read by, and can appeal to, fans anywhere and it is for these fans who may need a little introduction into these two fascinating football countries. Malaysia and Singapore are visited by many millions of people from around the world every year and both have sizable expat communities but when it comes to football, little is known outside Asia—except *kelong* (match-fixing), sadly.

This book is a loose attempt to find out if it is true and, if so, why. And even if the two countries are different, how much are they defined by their relationship to each other? And while there is obviously a shared history, how important is that today? This book is not an exhaustive history or a textbook but hopefully offers an interesting window on Malaysian and Singaporean football, with a look at their relationship both now and in the past.

And also, perhaps, the future. Is football in Malaysia and Singapore heading along the same path? *Lions and the Tigers* seeks to answer some of those questions, or at least explain why they can't be answered at all.

Fortunately you can find examples in very recent history to give those from outside the region a taste of what football in this part of the world is all about.

INTRODUCTION

THE AFF CUP AND THE PUSKAS AWARD— SUMMING UP FOOTBALL IN SINGAPORE AND MALAYSIA

They are a little more patient in Singapore football and they know that success does not usually come quickly. In Malaysia, we know that too, but we still demand it quickly.

—Zainal Abidin Hassan,
over 130 appearances for Malaysia from 1984–1996

On the morning of 7 October 2016, the rain was pouring in Singapore. The skies were darker than the looks on the faces of the Vietnamese players when R. Sasikumar's shoulder scored the decisive goal in the 1998 Tiger Cup final. It felt, well, like England, and it did not stop raining until late in the afternoon—something that did not bode well in terms of ticket sales at the new National Stadium. The build-up for the Friday night friendly clash with Malaysia was low-key, perhaps the lowest in recent memory. It was something of a disappointing feeling. The fallout from recent clashes in World Cup qualification and the AFF Suzuki Cup could still be felt, but this friendly was perhaps a one-off, a feeling that the two teams did not really want to be playing each other at that moment in time.

Both were dealing with issues of their own, and while it is pretty much always the case, this was more than the usual problems.

Malaysia were in all sorts of trouble and bringing a young squad that was desperate just to avoid defeat. In some ways, playing a young team was a wise decision. It meant that there was little pressure on the visitors and it was all on the hosts. A team that was in terrible form was going to field something of an experimental side. Any kudos that would come Singapore's way from winning the game was instantly reduced, especially as their line-up would be bursting with experience.

But overall, Singapore was in a better position in terms of form. Yet what they lacked in youth they did not make up for in excitement and flair. As legendary Singapore striker Aleksandar Durić told me, "there are many other things to do in Singapore", and while he was talking of youngsters preferring not to put on football boots, he could have been referring to this Friday night specifically.

Before the game, the atmosphere was flat. Such was the disillusion-ment across the Causeway that the travelling Malaysian fans barely numbered three digits. This was not going to be one of those derbies where the away section contributed to an unforgettable atmosphere. Not only that, but the ones that did make the journey were not in the highest of spirits. "A draw would be OK for us," said one who had made his way down from Melaka (unknowingly recreating my first journey to the city, though I will never know if he rushed through customs and immigration in the way I did on that first visit; probably he had plenty of experience in crossing the Causeway.) "We have lost so many games in the past few months, we really don't want to lose to Singapore. Beating them would be fantastic but I can't see that happening. For me, just don't lose and that is OK."

When you look at the record of the Tigers going into that game, it is easy to understand the lack of excitement around the national team. In 2015, there had been three 6-0 thrashings. And these were not against the giants of Asian football. Perhaps if it had been South Korea or Japan administering the beatings then it would have been a little easier to take. As it was, two humiliations came at the hands of Palestine and one against Oman. These were not minnows by any stretch of the imagination and had both reached the 2015 Asian Cup, but managed a combined total of three points in their six games. It was just embarrassing. Between the second Palestine loss in June, which came at home, and the upcoming game in United Arab Emirates, a much tougher opponent, I interviewed Malaysia coach Dollah Salleh. He vowed that by the end of the game in Abu Dhabi, Malaysia would do something to make everyone forget about the 6-0 losses.

And they did, but just not in the way that the coach had wanted. Malaysia went west and lost 10-0. UAE were a good team, finishing third at the 2015 Asian Cup, and nobody expected an away victory. Even so, it was a massive humiliation and one that Dollah, who kept his dignity on the sidelines and dealing with the media, was never going to be able to survive—and he didn't. Ong Kim Swee had been drafted in, getting the job at the end of 2015 on a temporary basis and then, after the Football Association of Malaysia had spent about three months looking for a permanent candidate, getting the nod full-time. In October 2016, the team were coming off the back of a 3-0 loss in Indonesia, the hosts' first international game for almost two years after being banned from international football by the good folks at FIFA who had allowed all kinds of craziness in Jakarta for years.

So the tiger that arrived in the Lion City was not a sleek predator full of hunger, confidence and menace but something of a scaredy-cat just looking to avoid defeat. And in the big rivalries that is sometimes what it is all about. Winning can be lovely but the prospect of standing—or these days sitting—in the stadium while watching rival fans celebrate wildly and lengthily is one of the worst feelings in football, despite how necessary it is from time to time.

"I was told that whatever you do, you must not lose to Malaysia," said Trevor Hartley when he arrived in 1976 to become Technical Director of the Football Association of Singapore (FAS) and then the national team coach shortly after. "Losing to Malaysia was a huge no-no. It was not just the people at the association or those working in football it was the media, of course, but also the people you saw on the street. When a game with Malaysia approached, people made it clear that defeat really was not an option. This is the one team you do not lose to. There was a lot of pride at stake."

And that pride was evident, even when the opponents were not the Harimau Malaya. "Even when Singapore played the Malaysian states, they really wanted to win," recalled Hartley. "There were a lot of bragging rights at the time. So when they played the Malaysian national team, the feeling was much bigger, of course. The media talked about it for days before the game and there was much more media. Not just the usual football writers, but everyone was talking about it. There was pressure on the players and the coach, it was good for everyone, as long as you did not lose."

It was the painful prospect of defeat as much as the potential delights of victory that make a derby such a big deal yet on 7 October it wasn't just the weather that had put a dampener on things. It was all a bit muted. There were not much more than 20,000 home fans in the 55,000-seat arena. The atmosphere started brightly, but the dourness of the game that eventually played out soon put as much a dampener on the Singapore evening as the rain had done in the day.

But still, but still, there was something. "We love nothing more than to beat Malaysia," said one fan who was just about to enter the stadium. "They are our neighbours and our rivals. For a Singaporean fan, there is nothing better than seeing them go home with nothing. That is just the way it is and I don't think that will ever change."

If the atmosphere was lacking, the desire of the two teams to win—or in Malaysia's case not to lose—was palpable. There was something out there on the pitch, there was a special feeling and, yes, there was a rivalry. With football currently at a fairly low ebb in both countries and the new National Stadium still a little unloved, there were still over 20,000 people ready to buy tickets and watch teams that were closer to 200 than 100 in the FIFA world rankings.

That something was there on the faces of the players after the game ended in a 0-0 draw. In the bowels of the stadium before exiting to the bus, the Malaysians passed through happy at negating the much more experienced hosts. Singapore were as frustrated as it is possible to be. "What an experience," said Malaysian debutant Darren Lok as he left the stadium. The English-born striker had been waiting for his Malaysian passport for months and had to wait until the second half for his introduction. He didn't score but worked his yellow-and-black socks off.

"It is great to come here to the home of our rivals to get a result. We are a young team," he said. "We made sure that we were not going to lose and we have come away with a good result."

He was right. For Malaysia, it was a good result. The reaction back home was OK. Fans did not seem to enjoy the football but understood the situation and at this moment in time, would tolerate such an approach.

Singapore captain Hariss Harun, a class act on and off the field who actually answers questions with thought instead of cliché, was still shaking his head at how Malaysia had escaped defeat.

"We've only ourselves to blame," were his words as he left. He would say something similar to me a few weeks later as Singapore exited the AFF Suzuki Cup in Manila, where the rain started during the game rather than ending just before. Yet the frown, the shake of the head and the general air of frustration and disappointment were pretty much the same.

Overall, the experience of this game did not match up to the tales of the past—the distant as well as the most recent. It was just, I was sure, bad timing and a combination of factors. But still, it was a good time to take stock, to look at the wider picture and what it all means. Is the rivalry the fiercest in the world? In football terms, surely not. Not even in Asia: South Korea and Japan probably win the continental title in that regard with their history, bitterness and long-standing position at the top of the Asian football tree. You could throw North Korea into that mix too, and there is no love lost between Saudi Arabia and Iran, or Saudi Arabia and United Arab Emirates. Others, such as India versus Pakistan, are more about their history and relationship off the pitch than anything significant in football terms. Singapore and Malaysia do have a fierce rivalry, but there is something else to it.

There is a shared history that is not bitter and brutal like Japan's relationship with Korea, but something deeper. There are surely few nations with the same relationship. They were both part of British-ruled Malaya for around a century and a half, that is six generations. Much shorter was the shared experience as part of the Federation of Malaya after the British left in 1957, ending when Singapore was expelled in 1965.

It is unavoidable, then, that there are close ties between the two countries. These were nations that were like brothers—with the requisite sibling rivalry—and sport, especially football, was an arena in which that could be played out.

I had hoped that it would be played out once again at the 2016 AFF Suzuki Cup, but I knew it was something of a forlorn hope. After all, they had been drawn in separate groups. At one time, that wouldn't have been such a big deal but such was the situation of the two teams going into the tournament that few expected that they would meet later. Perhaps one team might squeeze into the semi-finals, but both doing so was the kind of long shot that even Faiz Subri—more of him later—would struggle with.

In the end, both failed dismally and only won one game between them. That was Malaysia's slightly lucky win over Cambodia as they came from behind to win 3-2. At one time, such a close scoreline with the Angkor Warriors would not have gone down well with fans back home, but results were so bad over the preceding two years that supporters were happy to take what they could get. Subsequent defeats spelled the end. The first against Vietnam was expected; the second against co-host Myanmar should have been, even if it was not.

For the first time in the tournament's history, both nations exited at the group stage. The record books will show that Malaysia collected three points to Singapore's one, but it matters little. Both were out, and deservedly so.

ANOTHER SINGAPOREAN INQUEST

Singapore's failed AFF Suzuki Cup campaign in 2016 and its aftermath offer some insight into how football in the country works.

I was there in Manila on 25 November as the Lions left the Rizal Memorial Stadium and the tournament in a mild storm. The headlights of the waiting bus at the crumbling but atmospheric arena in the middle of the city not only illuminated the raindrops, but also the slump in the players' shoulders as they passed by an Indonesian press pack that were gleefully shouting "thank you" to the Lions as they walked past. It was hard to know if there was sarcasm or mockery in the greetings shouted out. It sounded like there was to me, but as they were not talking in their first language, I wouldn't say conclusively.

What could be said with complete confidence was that three games, one goal and one point meant failure and an early exit. It was not the finest hour for the four-time champions.

Coach V. Sundramoorthy had a few words after the game. As he was asked about his future by a journalist from the *New Straits Times*, the coach shot back: "How long have you been working there? Seventeen years? Did people judge you after six months?" (The journalist said nothing, but the obvious answer was "yes". As a writer, you are judged all the time, especially if you are freelance; six months can be quite a lengthy spell.) It was hard not to feel sorry for the coach who had to face the press in a media centre that was cramped and packed and, for some reason, did so alone with no official from the Football Association of Singapore (FAS) anywhere to be seen.

Singapore had left little mark on the tournament. Their football had been forgettable, barely noticeable. The team had gained just one point, and few friends on the pitch or off. The Lions were staying at the same Novotel Hotel in Cubao as their three group rivals, but had their own wing and did not share the same eating space as the teams from Thailand, Indonesia and the Philippines. At the end, most guests staying in the hotel barely noticed they left. Fans in the Philippines hardly noticed they arrived.

The country lacks some of the colourful chaos that can be found in Malaysian football, for better or for worse. Yet at such times, there is a well-worn debate about what the problem is and what should be done. It seems to me that there are few places in the world of football that worry so much about the future and talk so much about the past.

There have been concerns about the S-League for some time. The competition is a decent standard and offers professional football for the country's aspiring players to aim for, even if the average salary doesn't go far in Singapore (especially if you do your socialising around Clarke Quay).

But the league has become stale with attendances falling, which is understandable given the small population in the country. This makes the national team all the more important, and the sight of it struggling so much in a regional tournament that the country had, going into 2016, won four of the ten previous titles on offer was troubling. First round exits can happen, but this was different from 2014. There was little expectation that the Lions were going to make it and the team's performance reflected that, hoping to sneak into the last four.

This time there was some sympathy for the coach. After all, he had been given just a one-year contract by the FAS just six months earlier. There was little incentive to build for the future. Why bring in youngsters that would bear fruit for someone else years down the line? There was also little incentive to experiment with a different playing style.

Trevor Hartley was appointed as the coach of Malaysia in 1989 on a one-year contract with the sole purpose of leading the team to glory in the Southeast Asian Games. "They wanted me to bring in some young players, to change the team," said Hartley. "I wasn't going to do that in a year. The older players were still fine and I wasn't going to start bringing in a new generation when all they wanted was gold in Kuala Lumpur. I was going to be judged entirely on whether there was success at the SEA Games, so there was no reason for me to jeopardise the chances of winning that for building for a future in which I would not be around and would be completely changed anyway by the next guy."

It is hard to have your *rojak* and eat it: short-term success and long-term planning are not always mutually exclusive, but it takes more than a new coach to supply both. It takes a philosophy and determination throughout the football federation.

Sundram did what Hartley had done: put together a team that, he thought, was capable of winning here and now. A fine player in his day, he was not exactly noted for providing free-flowing football as a coach with Tampines Rovers, and so it proved with the national team.

The football was perhaps not quite as bad as some said; or at least, it would have been acceptable had results been better, and that was the sentiment I heard from the fans that had travelled to Manila. They felt that getting out of the group was the priority and that good football was a pleasant bonus. Singapore's pragmatism has served them well in the past.

While that sentiment was tested in the opening game—a goalless draw against the Philippines—it was always going to be a tough one coming against a confident co-host. It was made much tougher given the first half red card that was waved in the crestfallen face of Hafiz Sujad. Nobody will ever know what would have happened had he not kicked James Younghusband in the throat.

If I had been a Singaporean fan, however, the thing that would have worried me a little was not the fact that the four-time champs were hanging on against a team that had never been past the semi-finals before and had lost 19 out of 21 games in the tournament up until 2010, but the ease with which some observers seemed to accept the idea that Singapore would be happy with a point before kick-off.

As to which team was favourite, that was debatable. The Philippines were missing three of their foreign-based players, who had not been released by their clubs, but had performed well in the second round of qualification for the 2018 World Cup, famously defeating North Korea and Bahrain, two teams that may not be the cream of the Asian crop but were usually not that far below. Defeats in friendly games against the same opposition just a few weeks before had sowed the seeds of doubt, and while the Azkals were struggling a little, they were no longer the easy-beats of the past.

Singapore gave the co-hosts a little too much respect and there was a suspicion on my part—one that was dismissed by anyone I presented it to—that the sending off, while not welcomed, provided an excuse to sit back and not be too ambitious.

It is inadvisable to read too much into one game, but the second was more of the same, though perhaps understandably so in this instance. It ended with a 1-0 loss to Thailand, with the champions pressing in the final moments to score the vital goal. Singapore caused some problems and had chances to score and had the champions in trouble at times.

However, it was hard to escape the feeling that had the Lions been a little more aggressive and ambitious then they could have achieved a result against the best team in the region (and one that is leaving Singapore behind on and off the pitch too). We'll come back to Thailand a little later as the current strides being made by the "Land of Smiles" provides plenty of lessons and encouragement for everyone else in Southeast Asia, especially Malaysia and Singapore, who are supposed to be rivals on a similar level.

Daniel Bennett, Singapore's most capped international, also felt that the result could have been very different. "When we played them in the Suzuki Cup, they weren't as good as I expected. We could have beaten them had we a little more luck and we should at least have taken a draw from the game." The defender acknowledged that Thailand have moved ahead of the others in the region but was not overly impressed with the 2016 version. "They are obviously a good team with some talented players but I thought the Thai team from 2014 was stronger."

The final game was the most disappointing for the obvious reason that it was the last in the tournament, but there was more than that. Indonesia had impressed in the first two games, but still, Singapore expected to win against a team that was still recovering from a 12-month ban from international football by FIFA.

But talking to Indonesia coach Alfred Riedl before the game, he was not so sure about that. "They are playing a physical and defensive game," said the Austrian. "If it comes to a football contest then I think we can win. We know how to play against Singapore, the style of the team does not change that much," added the man who has been coaching in Southeast Asia on and off for two decades.

The Merah Putih's ("Red and White's") last competitive game before November 2016 had come two years earlier at the previous AFF Suzuki Cup. All seemed well when Khairul Amri volleyed the Lions into a first-half lead to score Singapore's first goal in the tournament. Yet after the break, the much-vaunted defence went walkabout twice and an energetic and inventive Indonesia took advantage to score twice.

When push came to shove, Singapore did not have the attacking talent to score the necessary goals against Indonesia and at vital times, the defence fell apart. Perhaps it was a small mercy that the Lions did not get through, as surely they did not have what it took to win the tournament.

What Singapore have, and what is one of their biggest strengths, is a certain pragmatism. This can be seen in the world of business, as the city state has developed into one of the financial hubs of not only Asia but the entire planet. Flexibility and taking advantage of opportunities is something that Singapore is good at.

And the same should be true in football. Had results been different in the Philippines, the football would have been glossed over. Talking to fans ahead of the opening game outside the stadium north of Manila, the message was: "Just get through the group stage, that is what we care about. Get to the knockout stage and anything can happen." It is hard to argue against that. While Thailand was the best team, being drawn in the same group meant that you couldn't face them in the semi-finals.

Just getting the right result against Indonesia—and given the way the group played out, a draw would have been enough for the last four—could have sent Singapore all the way to the final. But none of that came to pass. Singapore went home with one point and that meant criticism over the style of play was always going to be fierce. That is just the way it is in football.

Thailand coach Kiatisuk Senamuang has plenty of experience in Singapore as a player and against Singapore as a coach and player. He was not surprised at the way Singapore played. Lounging bare-chested by the pool at the Novatel in Cubao, he said this was just the country's style. "It is always this way," he shrugged. "Even when I was a player. Singapore defends and counterattacks while Thailand tries to pass the ball. The games always ended 1-0 or 2-1 or 1-1. This is the way it has always been. Singapore always plays this way. They do what they need to do to win. We do the same but in a different way."

It is hard to disagree. This is football and it would be boring if every team played in the same way, and while the styles of Thailand and Singapore were different on the pitch, the respective coaches were very different too. It is hard to imagine Sundram talking to reporters while lounging by the pool wearing just a pair of shorts. "Zico", as Senamuang was affectionately known, cut a relaxed and confident figure and was obviously enjoying himself, holding court. This was in contrast to his Singapore counterpart, who looked nervous and troubled as if he would rather be doing something else. Though it is striking that Zico was out of his job just three months later, the victim of his own success in Thailand as he raised expectations to an unsustainable degree, while Sundram stayed on. It just goes to show that you can never be certain of anything in football.

Yet there is something about Singapore football that reminds me a little of England. When the national team fails at an international tournament, the same inquest is held and the same conclusions are come to pretty much every time. There are the same worries about the direction the game is going in and the people who are in charge and about the nation's relationship with football in general.

Then what happens is that the anger fizzles out and is forgotten by the time the next games come around and the cycle starts again. If, as in Hinduism, the concept of time is that of a wheel that keeps turning and life keeps repeating itself, then the same is true in Singapore football, where the same debates keep rolling round again and again.

"The direction Singapore football needs to take must be set by football people. Instead you find bankers, lawyers and doctors running the game. I don't think that is right." This was Vincent Subramaniam talking in 2003. The national team coach at the turn of the century was discussing Singapore's failure at the 2002 Tiger Cup. Yet his words would not have sounded strange 13 years later after another group stage exit.

It came back to the age-old reason or excuse as to why Singapore can struggle to progress. "The football culture here is so different," said Subramaniam. "Our youngsters put football only third on their priority list, after studies and social activities. To succeed, aspiring footballers must sacrifice. A young footballer who wants to become a successful professional should be like a boy who goes into monkhood. If he cannot sacrifice the time and effort, then he should not consider it at all."

But youngsters are surely the product of the environment they grow up in. In January 2017, the Singapore Land Authority (SLA) told Home United Youth Football Academy that it was not to use two of its pitches at weekends or on weekday evenings. Local residents—well, five of them at least—found it all too loud and complained. One said that his son was struggling to study due to all the racket of young compatriots playing the beautiful game in the local neighbourhood. Studies come first in a country that leads the way in global education but does not seem quite so interested in getting up to international speed in football.

It caused quite a stir. Over two thousand people signed an online petition to protest SLA's decision. Jose Raymond, who had been a senior director at the Singapore Sports Hub, called the weekend and weeknight suspensions "a slap in the face for the development of sports culture in Singapore".

Mr Darryl David, deputy chairman of the Singapore government's Parliamentary Committee for Culture, Community and Youth, said:

"We shouldn't be focusing on the number of people making the complaint but the nature of it. These four people could be raising an issue that more are experiencing. I don't think this reflects on the community's attitude towards sporting culture."

Benjamin Tan is the former head of development at the Football Association of Singapore. Then he moved to Thailand to become Deputy CEO of the Thai Premier League and was concerned when he heard that youth academies were being told to restrict training times for children after complaints from local residents.

"Singapore has scarce land resources, so further deprivation of places for children to train is not good for the development of football in Singapore," Tan said. "It also may discourage other clubs from going to look at land to build academies or facilities. You need more opportunities for kids to play."

In Thailand, says Tan, it is not an issue. "It's not just because of land being more plentiful but because of the way society has changed," he explained. "With technology and all the iPads and iPhones that children play with, parents are happy to see them go and play outside and do something healthy and play sports, not just football."

Aleksandar Durić believes that things have deteriorated in Singapore football since he arrived in the nineties. "It has changed. Kids now are reading too much and they don't know how to make good talent. Coaches let their teams play bad football, they focus too much on improving fitness. You need to find a balance between technical ability and fitness, you can't just focus on one."

As well as youth development, there are also other issues. "The problem is that in the ASEAN region, coaches don't get time to show what they can do before they are fired. This is why football is the way it is in Southeast Asia. I am not sure if or when this trend will really change in this culture. Only the owners know why." Singapore is better than most in the region when it comes to patience with coaches, though that is hardly the highest of compliments. Durić would, however, still like the coaches to be a little tougher, stricter and harsher.

"They protect the local players too much, they make players who don't know how to play under pressure. Singapore is very small and it is hard to find good players. It is all connected though, as you can put too much pressure on and then you lose the young players. Singapore is a unique place—a mixture of study and army. It is something that is hard to understand if you are not from Singapore."

Perhaps more international coaches would help but Subramaniam had his doubts, disagreeing that European coaches were better than their Singapore counterparts just because European football is better. "Not every coach from Europe is good," said the former boss. "Some are as good, others are worse than local coaches. I would agree that the only area where Europeans may be ahead of Asians would be in team management and team-building. But knowledge, application of tactics and strategies, they are all universal and the development of footballers is also almost the same the world over."

Talking to his successor Jan Poulsen, it was obvious that not much had changed since the end of the last millennium. The Dane, who arrived in 1999 as the Director of the Goal 2010 Project, laughed, perhaps a little sadly, on hearing the story of Home United Youth Football Academy. He went on to explain how he ended up in Singapore.

"The story is like this. The Danish ambassador to Singapore at the time was at some kind of party and he was told by ministers about Project 2010. The ambassador is very interested in football, especially Arsenal. He said, 'Why not someone from Denmark?' And in this way, I made contact with the FAS. I applied for the job and I had to go to an interview and then they made the offer. I said 'thank you' and took the job. This was a government project."

Project 2010 was, said Poulsen, about laying the foundations in place so the Lions could go to South Africa in 2010—and not on safari, but to play at the World Cup. At the time, said the Dane, there were genuine hopes that it could be done. It may sound strange now as we know that Singapore finished third in their group behind Uzbekistan and Saudi Arabia but were nine points behind, taking points only off Lebanon. But then take Bahrain. This is a nation of just a few hundred thousand, compared to over five million in Singapore, has a league that struggles but came within a whisker of qualifying for the 2006 and 2010 World Cups. After being defeated by Trinidad and Tobago in the final play-off for Germany 2006, Bahrain expected to beat New Zealand to go to South Africa. Had they not missed a second half penalty in Wellington, that is exactly what would have happened. If a tiny Middle Eastern island with a population of not much more than Woodlands can do it, so can Singapore.

This seemed very far away in 1999. Asian federations have long been happy to target the third World Cup from the present, close enough to get people interested but far enough away to give plenty of room to manoeuvre. "This was my title, Project 2010 director," said Poulsen. "We wanted to participate in South Africa in 2010." He paused for a second. "(I)f I had known that I would have said no to the project. I would have said no because 2010 was almost impossible. Actually, it was impossible."

But these are debates that go back decades. In 1972, there was talk of how changes at the grassroots was going to give Singapore a solid foundation for years to come as Jeffrey Low wrote in *The New Nation* newspaper. "The dearth of local coaching talents will soon be arrested if plans by the Singapore Coaches Committee (SCC) works out without a hitch. A positive move has already been made to build a large pool of qualified and up-to-date coaches for all levels, from schools to clubs and constituencies." At the time, it was noted, there were 250 qualified coaches in the country, many of whom were not getting the support and direction they needed.

This was going to change over a period of four months, during which there would be five coaching courses held that would feed into an advanced trainers' course. This would provide a pool for the then national team coach Michael Walker to strengthen his coaching staff.

There was also another course devised for schoolteachers, to help them become better coaches as Major Abbas Abu Amin, chairman of the SCC, explained, "The schoolteachers course will be quite an important one because the coaches will be shown the right basics of football. They will be largely involved with students from 10 to 14 years old. That is why the teachers must teach the proper ways to young ones. If the students start on the right track from a tender age, it would not be such a great problem to correct minor faults. But if they develop bad habits from young, our task becomes greater when training future national potentials."

It all sounds reasonable, but it is not that hard to find similar talk almost half a century later. It suggests that not much has changed.

MALAYSIA GRAPPLES WITH A RARE TASTE OF GLOBAL ACCLAIM

Yet in the first few days of 2017 there was some news that suggested that the new year would be a lot better for football in the region than the old one. There was a hint that Southeast Asia could make waves on the world stage in a field that was not just about match-fixing.

A Malaysian won the Puskas Award. This was something to be truly proud of, though it turned into something a little controversial in the end. Malaysian football has a habit of snatching defeat from the jaws of victory and this happened, to a degree, with this global prize.

It started in a truly beautiful way. I was there in February 2016 when Penang midfielder Faiz Subri scored a truly amazing goal, a free-kick from 35 metres that swerved, dipped and swerved again to leave the Pahang goalkeeper as stunned as the watching fans. It also stunned those around the world as the goal went viral, with millions soon watching.

It was nominated by the Football Association of Malaysia (FAM) for the Puskas Award, the prize FIFA hands out for the most beautiful goal of the year. When voting opened online, the whole of the country's football fraternity voted and encouraged others to do the same. Even without that, the goal was spectacular enough to impress and it soon made the shortlist of ten and then the shorter list of three. Many felt that the strike was going to go all the way—the winner would be announced at a glittering ceremony in Zurich.

Penang and FAM fought over who could pay for the player to fly business class to the Swiss city. Tunku Ismail Sultan Ibrahim (TMJ), the president of Johor Darul Ta'zim FC, the champions of Malaysia, gave the player a cash prize—and then warned him, and the rest of the country, not to get too carried away with it all.

Faiz's rivals for the prize were both South Americans—one from Brazil, one from Venezuela. I met the player two days before he was making the journey. Penang coach Ashley Westwood (who was to last less than half a season) was not too happy at losing one of his players just a few days before the start of a new season but this was a Malaysian cause, something that the whole nation was getting behind, and something closely followed by the rest of the region.

The Puskas award may not be that big a deal in some parts of the world but this was a good news story on the international stage that Malaysian football was desperate for. In recent years, when Malaysia had made international news, the headlines were not happy ones, such as the two aviation tragedies suffered by Malaysian Airlines in March and then July 2014. Faiz going to Zurich marked a pleasant change.

Millions of people were looking forward to the ceremony. So was Faiz. He was genuinely excited and said with a smile that if there was any interest from Europe that he wouldn't mind signing for Manchester United. There was talk that he would wear a *baju Melayu*, a traditional

Malay outfit for men. He didn't, going for a suit and a bow tie instead.

As the tension and excitement built, the winner of the prize was announced by the original Ronaldo. The Brazilian striker was not quite as svelte in January 2017 as he was in his playing heyday, but then if a player has the career that he enjoyed then he should do what he likes. When he said Faiz's name, the Penang midfielder put his hands over his face, received a shoulder shake and a hug from FAM deputy-president Afandi Bin Hamzah (who was later criticised for "muscling in" on Faiz's photo with Cristiano Ronaldo) and then went to get the prize.

There was an awkward wait of quite a few seconds as the player searched on his phone and then gave a speech in broken English. Little could he have known that this would provoke a debate at home that would be in danger of overshadowing the award.

A writer for Malaysiakini, an online portal, lamented the appearance as embarrassing the country on the national stage. It was all part of a debate as to what it all meant for Malaysia.

Faiz's speech was compared with one given by Deputy Prime Minister Ahmad Zahid Hamidi at the United Nations in September 2016 at the United Nations. Then the politician was criticised at home for speaking "Manglish", a Malaysian version of English with a local pronunciation of some English words. Many felt that he, like Faiz, should have spoken Malay as a matter of principle anyway, as there were translators available. Others lamented that it marked a general decline in the English-speaking ability of Malaysians.

"Time was when Malaysians were complimented on the standard of their English; now it is the stuff of embarrassment, not infrequently on the international stage, before a global audience," went the article. "To be sure, Malaysian football and other sports fans are delighted by Faiz's achievement in winning the Puskas award. However, if they watched the footage of his moment in the spotlight, whatever pride they must have felt over Faiz being chosen as winner would have been diminished by his shambling performance on being called to receive the prize and say a few words."

It seems harsh to compare the acceptance speech of a football player that will probably happen once in a lifetime, if that, to that given by an experienced politician who is obviously accustomed to public speaking.

It was also harsh and it was certainly unfortunate that the player was asked about this on his arrival at Kuala Lumpur airport after a long flight from Zurich.

"People are going to speak whatever they want, I can't control that," he said at a press conference. "I do not mind the criticism, as I've done my best and my target after this is to do better for myself and Pulau Pinang," he said.

Minister of Youth and Sports Khairy Jamaluddin was a bit more forthright: "They (the critics) should not have focused on such a trivial matter, instead they should have focused on Faiz's effort and the recognition he has brought to the country. For me these critics are those who have never received any international awards like what Faiz has achieved."

It was unfortunate for the player, who should not have had to deal with any of those barbs, but the episode gives an idea of what makes Malaysia such a fascinating and intriguing place. Not many countries could turn what should have been a universally acclaimed moment into a national debate about a different matter entirely. The prize will forever be Faiz's and completely deserved, and he should treasure it.

CHAPTER 1

THE EARLY DAYS:
SINGAPORE, SELANGOR, PENANG
AND THE MALAYSIA CUP

I grabbed the chance to show what an Asian could do with a football.
And did it well.

—Lim Yong Liang, Singapore striker, 1922–1934

In 1944, the British ship HMS *Malaya* was used as a target ship for
prototype bouncing bombs in Loch Striven in Scotland. She had had
a busy World War II, escorting convoys and facing the Italian navy in
the Mediterranean Sea, as well as shelling the city of Genoa in 1941.
The vessel was attacked and damaged in the same year near Cape Verde,
but limped into a Caribbean port before returning to fitness to escort
convoys cross the Atlantic.

Previously, she had done three things of historic note. She was
involved, just a year after she was constructed in Newcastle, in the
Battle of Jutland in 1916, the biggest naval engagement of World War I
and the only meeting between the main fleets of the British Royal Navy
and the Imperial German Navy. The ship suffered heavy damage and
65 people died. The vessel also carried the last Sultan of the Ottoman
Empire, Mehmed VI, from Istanbul to exile on Malta in 1922. And a
year earlier—in January 1921—HMS *Malaya*, so named because it was
built by money provided by the government of British-ruled Malaya,
had visited the country that it was named after.

The ship called at Port Swettenham, Singapore, Melaka, Penang and
Port Dickson, with the crew playing locals in all kinds of games including
football, rugby, golf and hockey. Not long after the ship departed back
to Europe, the captain, H.T. Buller, sent a letter to the Chief Secretary
of the Federated Malay States in which he offered to send two cups,
one to be competed for in rugby and the other in football, as a token

of gratitude at the warm welcome the vessel had received upon its visit.

This was called the Malaya Cup and then later became known as the Malaysia Cup, one of the most historic cup competitions in the world—and surely one of the best and most loved. The skipper of the ship could not have dreamed this would be the longest-lasting contribution to world history that his charge would ever make.

That original trophy lasted until 1967, when the Football Association of Malaysia created the Malaysia Cup. The first final had taken place 46 years earlier between Selangor and Singapore, two rivals that were going to meet plenty of times again over the years. Of the rivalry that exists between the two countries, a fair proportion can be ascribed to this special relationship between the Red Giants and the Lions.

1 October 1921 had started wet, but by kick-off at the Selangor Club, conditions had improved somewhat and the crowd was looking forward to what was expected to be a very good game of football and a splendid social occasion.

Singapore had defeated Negri Sembilan and Melaka along the way to becoming South Zone champions. Selangor represented the North Zone by virtue of downing Perak and thrashing Penang 5-1.

The Straits Times seemed excited:

"The crowd was probably the largest ever for a football match in Malaya," the newspaper reported. "People from Penang, Perak, the Province, Seremban, Malacca, Singapore and the districts of Selangor thronged the field. Along the touchline on the side of the club, seating accommodation was provided for about 200 people. But by 4.30pm, all the seats were occupied and there was a requisition for more seats. All the four sides of the ground were crowded with a dense mass of people five and six deep. An improvised jazz band, with Lt. Riches as the guiding genius, relieved the tedium of waiting."

Selangor won the toss and kicked-off at 5 p.m. Singapore started the brighter. The Lions were made up of plenty of British military and had one Asian in the side, the dangerous Chee Lim, who was pushing and probing in attack.

Jamieson, a Scot, broke the deadlock just before the break, with a shot that, according to the newspaper, "could have beaten the best custodian in the region."

Selangor also had plenty of Brits on the pitch and Rozario equalised for the Red Giants around the hour mark. But it was Moss who scored the winning goal five minutes before the end and it was left to the Lions to lift the trophy—plainly adorned, according to reports. The game ended 2-1 to Singapore, starting a long love affair for the Lions with the competition. Celebrations were enthusiastic by Singapore supporters at the venue but the Malaya Cup was just starting to make emotional inroads back home.

Selangor took revenge the following year but the Lions bounced back to win the next three. From then, the two rivals almost took turns to keep the trophy, and actually shared the prize in 1928 and 1929. In 1930, Johor and Kedah joined the Malaya Cup and two years later, the Football Association of Malaya (FAM) took over the operation of the competition.

Singapore won the 1941 trophy, the last one until 1948 due to the intervention of World War II. By that time, with the Japanese poised to invade, Singapore had won 12 cups from 1921 compared to five for Selangor, with two shared trophies. Only Perak broke the duopoly with two wins, but it was Singapore that dominated, appearing in every final from 1921 to 1941. It was, and remains, a highly impressive achievement. There can be few tournaments that have been, for a time at least, so closely identified with one team.

One of the major figures from that era of almost total Singaporean domination was Lim Yong Liang. The man known as "Pop" has few rivals for the title of the best striker that Singapore has ever produced. He began his career at the age of 15, starting out for the Chinese junior side. In 1922, he was chosen to represent Singapore in the Malaya Cup in just its second ever edition and was still there in 1928, appearing in all the competition's finals except in 1924, and scoring three goals along the way. This was a striker who could play anywhere in the forward line. In 1928, he also led the Singapore Sino-Malay team, which surprised local fans and journalists by defeating a decent Australian eleven. The Aussies were extremely impressed.

Lim was recalled in 1934, helping the team to the title once again. Perhaps he could have taken the moniker of the "Singaporean Gary Lineker" (or for chronology, perhaps the former Barcelona and England striker could be called the "English Lim Yong Liang"), as he had a knack for popping up in the penalty area at the right time and right place to score and was also known for always staying on the right side of the referee. In 1947, the Singapore Free Press newspaper noted that "old soccer fans cannot recall an occasion when he was pulled up for ungentlemanly conduct on the field." It is hard to say with certainty, but it was extremely unlikely that Lim ever defecated on the pitch as the English striker had during a World Cup match in 1990.

The "Grand Old Man" of Singapore football was a little envious of Fandi Ahmad, one of the few rivals for the title of best ever striker from the country, and the opportunities he had in the eighties. "I grabbed the chance to show what an Asian could do with a football. And I did it well," he said in 1980. "How I wish I were 25 years old again and at my peak and staring at an Ajax contract." He died two years later. Looking back, Lim offers a classic case of "what if". The British players who were active at the time all felt that Lim was good enough to play for clubs in England, but it was just not a realistic option at the time.

Lim's advice to Fandi was to try to join one of the giants of European football. "This is the chance that Fandi must grab. Forget about Niac [from Indonesia], go to Europe and show what an Asian can do with the ball."

Lim was to continue to be a major figure after hanging up his boots, going on to coach all Singapore's Malaya Cup teams from 1936 to the outbreak of war in 1941. He then went on to spend more than two decades as the secretary at the Singapore Amateur Football Association (SAFA). He claimed in an interview with *The Straits Times* that he had seen almost all the 348 games that had taken place in the Merdeka Cup. "I have seen 'em all except one series in 1966 when I went to London to see England win the World Cup at Wembley. It has always been my ambition to see as much as I can of all the English soccer teams and at last, I am about to fulfill that ambition before I get too old."

He also continued to watch Singapore in the Malaysia Cup and in 1976 went to the dressing room to console the Lions, who had lost to Selangor in the final. "What are all these people crying about? So what if we lost? Next year, we'll win it. So I must start now to encourage the players." Such common sense and clarity of thought would be welcome these days, too. And Singapore did win it the next year.

Lim was a giant of those early years and played a huge part in the development of Singapore football, as well as the Malaya/Malaysia Cup, but the arrival of the Japanese was also influential.

The last final before war finally broke out in the region took place on 16 August 1941. By this time, there were fewer British players in the local sides—they were needed elsewhere—though they were obviously well represented when it came to the RAF and Army teams. The players that came from the United Kingdom were not the best but a few top talents did arrive, such as Johnny Sherwood, an outside left who played for Reading in the 1941 War Cup Final. Regardless, the Brits did not enjoy losing to the improving local teams, believing that it went against the established order. After all, who invented the game and who ran the country?

In 1941, the RAF and Army teams finished below Singapore—by now made up solely of local players—in the group stage of the southern zone. Again losing to the locals did not go down well and the British consoled themselves by telling all who would listen that their football was still the best—the lessons that Hungary would give in 1953 at Wembley were still some time away.

Singapore then went to the final against Penang. Lai Chuan gave the Lions the lead. Penang, not yet known as the Panthers, had three talented Brits, with goalkeeper Cyril Gibbons, left-back Cyril Ashmore and the man who equalised for Penang after 20 minutes, striker Frederick Askew. Yet Singapore's skipper Aziz was a towering presence at centre-back and repelled all attacks. Goals from Taib and Quan Chong settled it and Singapore took title number 12 in a competition that they had come to love.

Shortly after, the Japanese army arrived in Penang. It was symbolic. This island was the first British territory in the whole of Southeast Asia and was first occupied in 1776. Then, 165 years later, the colonisers abandoned the "Pearl of the Orient" in a panic without firing a shot. The Japanese continued down the peninsula towards Singapore. British and Commonwealth troops provided some resistance this time, but not enough. With the Japanese occupying the Malay peninsula and Singapore, local football was obviously not a priority.

While the war ended in 1945, the Malaya Cup did not get going again until 1948. Perhaps the other states were just not that excited about being on the receiving end of more Singaporean domination. It can't have been much fun for the others in the pre-war period when Singapore reached the final every single time.

The return to action in the southern section saw Singapore defeat Johor 4-1 and normal service looked like it was going to be resumed. There was then a 3-0 win over Army/Navy and then a 2-2 draw with the Royal Air Force (RAF). But something strange happened in the fourth game. Singapore lost, and not only that, lost at the Jalan Besar Stadium. The historic date was 19 June 1948, and the Lions were defeated by Negri Sembilan, who went on to lift the trophy, beating Selangor in the final after a replay. It was only the third time that the cup had gone to neither Singapore nor Selangor.

But back to the first defeat in the group stage, a first such loss in 73 games. It was a defeat that almost sent the city into meltdown. Mr F.C. Sands was the president of SAFA and was at a loss to explain what happened, as *The Straits Times* reported. "I have never seen Singapore play so badly; every player seemed to be off form. However, the fitter team won and I offer my congratulation to Negri Sembilan for their creditable victory."

For a team that was not accustomed to losing when it mattered, they accepted defeat in a gentlemanly manner.

The shock win was not undeserved. The hosts started well, but it did not take too long for the visitors to settle. Once they did, they took the game to Singapore and scored after ten minutes, with Soon Teck heading home the opener after an inswinging free-kick delivered by Thian Kwee. Though Singapore equalised from the spot, a striker called, simply, Captain Watson struck in the second-half, one in which the team known as NS dominated.

"We played hard," said Watson. "This is a historic win and we are delighted that we can be the first to win here in the group. We all pulled together as we know that Singapore always get to the final. It shows that if you work hard then the strongest team can be defeated."

What was generally agreed by all who watched the game was that the powerhouse of peninsular football had underestimated their opponents. "The real reason," said the hard-hitting columnist known as "Crusader" in the Singapore Free Press, "lay in the fact that the Singapore players, like their supporters, did not give a serious thought to the possibility of defeat. After all, it was only little Negri Sembilan...why train, why bother."

The Straits Times reflected the general feeling by saying that a full-strength NS team playing to the best of its ability would be happy with a draw. The paper was right—until they were proven wrong.

It wasn't quite the blip that fans in Singapore were hoping for, though the performance in 1949 was a bit better. Singapore didn't make the final for the second year running and the second year in the competition's history, but this time only lost out on goal difference to the Army/Navy team.

Normal service was resumed in 1950. Singapore won the cup for the first time since 1941, and that triumph signalled the start of a fruitful period of seven appearances in the next seven finals.

And there was plenty to write about in those games. It was a golden time for the competition.

HERE COME PENANG—AND YEARS OF CONTROVERSY

If only Melaka had been a power at the time, then the three-way relationship could have been called the "Straits Settlements Rivalry". But for a few exciting years, it was all about Penang and Singapore, two places that had historically plenty in common but were about to build a football history together too.

There had been meetings in 1934 and 1941 when Penang lost the final to Singapore. But the fifties was when it really got going. After the two years without a final appearance, Singapore won all their group games in 1950 and met Penang in the final for a third time.

Because of the two previous defeats, Penang was desperate to win the trophy and saw home advantage as, well, a major advantage. The Penang FA president Yeap Hock Hoe offered to shoulder all of Singapore's expenses for a trip that seems short now but was still a bit of a trek back then. Air tickets were offered, as were first class hotels. Yeap met his SAFA counterpart at the races and made his offer, but W. McGregor Watt was not impressed at the prospect of handing over home advantage to the northerners.

Had Singapore not just suffered the indignity of sitting out of the last two finals, perhaps they would have been more open to the idea of playing a one-off game in the Pearl of the Orient. But Singapore had pulled out all the stops to ensure that they did not record an unwanted hat-trick. The team was criticised for resting players for other competitions so they would be fresh for the Malaya Cup—an early form of rotation.

But Penang were confident. After a win over Perak in the group stage, the team could start to look forward to the final. Yeap was especially delighted. "I am more than happy by the display of our Penang boys," he said. "They played great soccer and if they play as they played today we have every chance of winning the trophy for the first time."

There was much expectation on the shoulders of star striker Abu Baidah. He scored all five goals in the thrashing of Perak not long before, and was in great shape after returning from injury. "We know that Singapore are a strong team and have won the cup many times," he said. "We are still looking for a first trophy. It is important that we win."

In the end, Penang did not get their way and had to play a one-off game in Kuala Lumpur. Special bus services were laid on for fans. They were disappointed once again. Singapore won 2-0 to make it three final wins out of three between the two teams and a first since 1941.

The venue for the final was often a bone of contention. In 1951, Singapore confirmed that they were back as a force and won it again, this time thrashing Perak 6-0. But they were insistent that the final should be played at Jalan Besar.

As the holders, they felt that they had the right to host the game, as the last time the final had been played at the arena was back in 1938. The State Associations were not happy with the idea and felt that playing in Singapore would give the hosts a home advantage worth one or two goals. SAFA were ready to offer a substantial share of the gate receipts to Perak but just like in 1950 and Penang, Perak were just as desperate to win the cup and did not want to give Singapore, already favourites, a greater chance of winning.

In the end, Singapore had to play the final in Kuala Lumpur and, boy, did they play. It only served to inspire the visitors and they thrashed Perak 6-0 in front of about 9,000 fans. It was a dominant display from start to finish. Perak's captain was Jack Crossley, who had once played for Hull City, and he pointed out the problem that the northerners brought upon themselves. "Perak dribbled the ball instead of moving it," he said, referring to his team in the third person (an unusual thing to do—almost as unusual as modern players dissecting their team's tactics in post-match interviews).

Just as he did not stop running in the game, he went on to give more of his opinion. "They could not settle down and were outplayed. Singapore were by far the superior side and had better stamina. They played grand football." Singapore were also fitter and better organised, and in the words of the *Singapore Free Press*, "played more forceful and scientific football" to knock Perak off their stride.

There had been some that felt Perak could win the trophy for the first time since 1931 when they had defeated Singapore 3-1 in the final. Khoo Kai Swee, former honorary coach of the Selangor Chinese Recreation Club, predicted a Perak triumph due to the fact that Singapore's defence was weak, especially with the threat posed by Crossley.

He was prescient in pointing out that Singapore's Chia Boon Leong, who had represented China at the 1948 London Olympics and in 1954 won a prize of a month's training in England and time with Arsenal after being voted as Malaya's most popular football player, was dangerous. He said something similar about star centre-forward Awang Bakar.

"[Boon Leong] is a brainy player and creates beautiful openings for other forwards. He was known to lack stamina but according to reporters, he has had sustained and strenuous training." Boon Leong, who stood at not much more than five feet tall, was identified as the man of the match by many, which is doubly impressive considering Awang Bakar grabbed a hat-trick.

What was also notable was that this was labelled the most eagerly awaited of all the post-war finals. Local hotels were all full, though the September weekend fell around the same time as the Selangor races, and over 100 police and military personnel were to be on hand to ensure that a full house did not become dangerously overcrowded. In the end, the most dangerous thing on display in Kuala Lumpur was the Singapore attack, which delivered the trophy once again.

In 1952, Penang were back on the scene and hoping that it would be fourth time lucky against Singapore. Despite the losing record, there were high hopes for the October clash. It turned out to be one of the most exciting and best finals in history.

Both teams had chances in a breathless first half, but it was Singapore that took the lead against the run of play. It was a spectacular strike and befitting such an occasion, with star striker Awang Bakar, who was to play a major part in this fixture over the years, scoring an overhead kick to send the 300 or so Singapore fans in the Perak stadium wild with delight. Awang was a class act and deserves to be better known in Southeast Asia than he is.

Penang turned up the pressure but just couldn't find a way through, and the chant "Lucky Singapore" started to ring around the Chinese Assembly Hall ground. Just before the break, however, Pang Siang Teik scored the equaliser. Soon after the restart Aziz Ahmad, who had made the equaliser, added a second to put the Panthers in the lead—and the fans started to believe that it could finally happen, that the cup was going to Georgetown for the first time. They pushed forward looking for a third but Rahim Omar headed home the equaliser instead.

With 15 minutes remaining, it was 2-2 and anyone's game. It was settled by a disputed goal. Rahim turned provider and swung the ball over, and there was Awang to head home his second and his team's third.

There were protests that the striker had used his hands. The defenders and fans had their hands in the air trying to get the referee to change his mind. It didn't work.

What must Penang have thought of Singapore? Four times they had met in the final and four times the Lions had won. What had Penang done to deserve such a nemesis? As the fans made the relatively short journey home from Ipoh, there was a feeling that it was never going to happen, that Penang's name was never going to be on the cup.

But they were back, and so was the optimism, a year later. Yes, Penang met Singapore for the fifth time in the final in 1953. Once again, Singapore tried to have the game played at home, but once again the effort was unsuccessful. The SAFA wrote to Penang FC, suggesting two alternative proposals. The first suggestion was a home-and-away leg, the second a good old-fashioned coin toss decided where the final would take place.

Penang held a two-hour emergency meeting to deliberate on the matter before deciding to turn down the proposals. There was some debate, however. Singapore had pointed out that the cup final had not been held in either of the two islands for two decades. It was time to at least let one set of home fans witness the game. Some Penang officials were interested in the idea of a home-and-away game, especially if they could host the second leg at home; and financially, it had a certain appeal.

In the end, however, they preferred to stick to the original plan set out by the Football Association of Malaya, and that was to play the game once again in Ipoh on 22 August. The fact that Ipoh is relatively close to Penang perhaps swayed the argument. You could get there and back on the same day, even in the days before the North–South Expressway cut the journey to not much more than an hour.

The first 400 tickets given to Penang sold out within minutes and not long after it was clear that of the over 4000 seats sold at the Chinese Assembly Hall ground, more than half would be occupied by Penang backsides. Hotels in and around the city filled up quickly. You can't say that fans of the Panthers were pessimists. They refused to believe that they were never going to win.

Once again Awang Bakar was seen as the danger-man for Singapore in attack; but there was hope in the north that their own star attacker, Pang Siang Teik, could make a difference.

Singapore had stumbled the week before the final, losing to Kluang, but coach Dick Pates was able to explain that away. "I make no excuses for our loss. We were deservedly beaten but I did tell our players before the game to avoid any possible injury." Pates promised that his boys would be ready to administer the now customary defeat to Penang in the final.

Singapore were full of confidence. After all, Penang should really have beaten their rivals in the final the previous year, but failed to do so. It seemed that the southerners, with their four wins in four finals against the team from the north, had the hex over their rivals. And Singapore had the knack of being able to win big games, even when they were not playing well. This was something that Penang lacked.

If Singapore were confident, there was also something in Penang's favour. Penang FA president See Seang Hua looked around at what was happening in the world to see that 1953 was a year of firsts. Mount Everest had been conquered, Stanley Matthews had finally collected an FA Cup winner's medal and later that year England would lose to Hungary at Wembley, a first defeat to foreign opposition on home soil.

If these events could finally come to pass, then there was no reason why Penang could not lift the Malaya Cup for the first time. It also seemed as if it was fate that kept bringing Penang and Singapore together in the final. Like any good computer game, to get the big prize, you have to defeat the big boss.

The feeling in Penang was that the only team that could beat them was themselves. If they settled quickly and were not affected by nerves then the trophy would be heading northwest after the game for a party that had been decades in the making.

Excitement was boosted by good news from Ipoh. While there had often been too much rain ahead of past finals, there were concerns that weeks without rain had left the pitch in Perak dry and dangerous. The day before the game, the heavens opened for 45 minutes, the first downfall for 20 days.

Singapore coach Pates was hedging his bets before the game. "I am never confident of winning any match but I am confident that our players and reserves are fit, are members of one happy family and will do their utmost to win. I would say that our team is as strong as that of last year but not as strong as the previous year when we won the cup final against Negri Sembilan by six goals to nil.

"If we are beaten by Penang we have no excuses. But I am sure every member of the team will do his utmost and it will not be through lack of trying if we failed to succeed." He added that there had been a special preparation programme implemented in the weeks leading up to it.

"For the last three weeks intensive training has been carried out at Jalan Besar stadium—every other evening after six o'clock for at least an hour. In addition, they have had massages at the stadium. Certainly, no other Malaya Cup team has ever had the same opportunities of getting physically fit."

Amid a raucous atmosphere at the Chinese Assembly Hall, Singapore took the lead in the twentieth minute with Ismail Yusoff running onto an Aw Boon Seong pass to shoot past Swee Hock. It seemed to Penang that history was repeating itself but this time, they were made of sterner stuff than in the previous four finals.

Three minutes before the break, Siang Teik equalised from a corner, and the sigh of relief around Ipoh was palpable.

Penang had looked to neutralise the threat of star Singapore striker Awang Bakar by deploying their own forward, Yah Hin Hean, back into defence to cover. It worked. Two goals in the first five minutes of the second half won the game and a first-ever cup for Penang. Aziz Ahmad put the team ahead and two minutes later Siang Hock extended the team's lead. Ismail pulled a goal back for Singapore, coming close to getting the equaliser and his hat-trick, but Penang held on for a famous 3-2 win.

There was some controversy. Singapore had appeared in six of the previous eight finals and had won them all. This was a team accustomed to winning on the big stage and especially comfortable with facing Penang. The loss hurt. Soh Ghee Soon, the Singapore team manager, said a few words at a special post-final dinner that was supposed to be a celebration party but instead provided a platform for an impromptu inquest.

"I do not begrudge Penang victory," he said. "But I feel that if all our players pulled their weight, we would have won. If any of them have a conscience about the part they played in the game, I leave them with it." Most felt that he was referring to a player or players who had "sold the game". So much for the coach's pre-match assertion that there would be no excuses if Penang won.

Some fans did not take too kindly to the manager blaming the players for the loss. A letter, signed "THREE-TWO (SQUARED)" from Penang to *The Straits Times* advised him to take the beating like a man. "It is rather ungrateful on your part after they struggled so heroically, although they lost. There is even honour in losing.

"Furthermore, don't blame the ball or the weather or the last breakfast and above all don't blame Penang for the 'tactics' they adopted during the last ten minutes … The fact remains that Penang was superior and so Singapore had to bow down to the worthy victors. Better luck next year Singapore."

The tactics in question had been highlighted by the Singapore press and were labelled as being unsporting with Penang, especially captain Cheng Eng, eager to run down the clock, as well as being a little more physical than Singapore would have liked.

Penang didn't care and who could blame them? This was a state that had been so close to glory on four previous occasions but had lost all four, and all to the same team. The feeling was that if Singapore were unhappy about the way Penang closed out the match, then tough. Singapore could take solace in the 17 trophies they had already won.

The Penang players returned home the next day to be greeted as heroes, as thousands lined the streets. The island and the surrounding state partied for days as the drought had finally been broken.

Yet this particular mini-series had not come to an end. Just as Penang had sought revenge over Singapore in the past for their final defeats, Singapore had their opportunity in the following year as the two teams met in the final of the 1954 edition.

Penang were favourites—though only just—and there wasn't the usual talk of trying to get the game played on either island. Singapore were determined to go and play wherever the game may be and the location was Kuala Lumpur. The Lions flew by air.

Coach Pates was still there, as were star attackers Boon Leong— Malaya's Footballer of the Year—and Awang Bakar. This time, though, there was young Rahim Omar, who was becoming a real star of the team. Singapore wanted to bring the trophy back to its rightful place and there was certainly plenty of attacking talent.

This time round there were no complaints, no ambiguity or what-ifs. It ended up 3-0 to Penang and there was little of the tension that had been evident the year before, when the Panthers were hanging on to a 3-2 lead with their claws, fangs, tail—whatever they had. There was some controversy, however.

In the ninth minute, Rahim Omar confirmed his star potential by scoring from a corner to stun Penang fans. Unfortunately for Singapore, it was ruled out as it was adjudged that the swerving ball had gone out of play before returning into the area for the striker to score. It was the first occasion that Penang goalkeeper Dave Maclaren was beaten in the game and, as perhaps the best shot-stopper in Malaya at the time, there was not going to be a second. He was pretty much perfect after that, and was helped by the fact that Penang central defender Yap Hin Hean had Awang Bakar in his pocket for almost the entire game.

Awang was, and still is, one of the best players in the history of Singapore. He loved the Malaya Cup and scored goal after goal, year after year. If he drove Penang defenders and fans mad with frustration, it was the opposite in Singapore. He was a popular footballer.

In the 1955 competition he scored seven goals, including one in the final against Kelantan as Singapore took the trophy back, but soon after he began to have fitness issues. And the career that had given pleasure to millions and pain to quite a few opposition defenders and fans was coming to an end.

Rahim looked to be the new star. The left-winger used to practice shooting balls barefoot through the spokes of a bicycle wheel in Farrar Park, historically a fertile breeding ground for talent. There he was spotted by a local coach and signed up to Fathul Karib FC.

Rahim's exploits off the pitch were almost as colourful as those on it, with his private life attracting plenty of attention. This was never more so than in 1969 when he stood trial after being accused of bigamy.

He married Caroline de Cruz in May 1956 and then went on to wed Hamidah binte Arshad in 1967. De Cruz, the accuser, claimed that he had left their home for Kuala Lumpur in January 1967 and never returned. "He wrote me a letter saying he did not want to have anything to do with me and our four children," she said in court. "He said that all those years he had waited to marry one of his own kind." After he left for KL, his first wife said that he had sent money for two months, but that was it. "He wrote me a letter asking permission to remarry. I refused him because we were not married according to Muslim rites."

She went to Kuala Lumpur, obtained his certificate for his second marriage and made a complaint to court. After the two-day trial, Rahim was cleared of bigamy, as the court ruled that Muslim law would not recognise the first marriage and therefore the second was valid. Judge Alexander went on to say: "I order Rahim to be acquitted and discharged without his defence being called."

It was a close call and Rahim was seen as something of a wayward football player. When the mood took him, he could be devastating but the mood did not always take. Coach Choo Seng Quee was one of those coaches who was able to get the best out of him; perhaps the player just responded to a firm hand, and Choo's hand was nothing if not firm.

Rahim was quite a character, of the sort that we don't see these days. For one thing, he was willing to openly challenge fans that abused him in the stadium and there are tales of him standing in front of supporters and trading insults. There are also tales that Singapore FA officials used to bribe his opponents on the billiards tables on the day of big games. They wanted them to let Rahim win so that he would arrive at the stadium in a good mood, although it may have been better to let him lose to take his frustrations out on the football pitch. At the very least, there were occasions when officials would personally go to the billiards halls and drag the star to the Jalan Besar Stadium just in time for kick-off.

The story could have gone very differently. He almost became one of the very first Asian players to play in Europe. In 1956, Portsmouth tried to sign the player. Pompey boss Eddie Lever wrote to Bob Pidgeon, president of Singapore league club Argonauts, asking about the then 22-year-old's availability. He had heard on the grapevine—a pretty good grapevine in those days—that this was a talent who could thrive in England.

At that time, Rahim was ignoring invitations to join up with Singapore's training squad and was not appearing in club football either. He was keen to head to England's south coast, however. "I'd like to get a chance in England. But I can't afford to get there under my own steam." It never happened, just as a move to Luton Town had fallen through the previous year as the player could not get the funds together.

It was a shame and perhaps things would have been very different had he been able to make the journey. Not only for the man himself, but for football in Singapore and even Southeast Asia. Had there been a Southeast Asian who made a name for himself in England in the late fifties and early sixties then perhaps history would have turned out differently, though it would not have been easy. Rules in England at the time stated that non-British players had to be resident in the country for two years before being able to play. It is unclear if the striker knew that but even so, time would have been on his side had he been able to make it west.

We will never know but it was clear that by the mid-fifties, Singapore's dominance of the competition was also coming to an end. The team still won trophies—seven more before it exited the tournament in the nineties—but was not as much of a fixture in the final as in the past.

But before the exit, the Lions reacquainted themselves with Selangor as the two teams enjoyed some titanic clashes in the seventies and early eighties.

CHAPTER 2

THE SIXTIES, SEVENTIES AND THE SINGAPORE AND SELANGOR SERIES

Selangor were literally laughing in the rain at Singapore's lack of resistance!

—Karl-Heinz Weigang, former Malaysian national coach

While the Singapore and Selangor rivalry really caught fire again in the mid-seventies, there was a momentous meeting in 1965 and this was special because of off-the-field issues. The final between the two teams took place just nine days before the great separation, before Singapore was to secede from the Federation of Malaya and become an independent sovereign nation.

There had been a lot of talk about what the separation would mean in the sporting arena. Just before the final, Kwok Kin Keng, the president of the FAM, put minds at ease by saying that Singapore would continue to be invited to participate in the Malaysia Cup, comments that were welcome across the Causeway amid concerns that Singapore would have to re-enter the international sporting arena.

Ahead of the uncertainty, another Malaysia Cup final between Singapore and Selangor was a welcome piece of familiarity. It was a strong Singaporean team that went to meet the Red Giants, the first final clash between the two at the Merdeka Stadium.

Selangor dominated the first half and took the lead eight minutes before the break, but the soon-to-be foreigners hit back with three goals in the second half to give coach Choo Seng Quee another triumph. To have the trophy sitting in Singapore as it became an independent nation must have been welcome.

In England, the seventies were a time of national team underperformance but a time when clubs started to dominate European competitions. It was a time of long-haired, maverick magicians who battled for supremacy with, usually, short-haired, hard men who loved nothing more than to chop "fancy Dans" down to size.

There was plenty of hair in this corner of Southeast Asia too, and when fans in Malaysia and Singapore talk of the golden age, especially in the former's case, they are often talking of the seventies. And when it came to the Malaysia Cup, still the biggest deal in town, it was all about Selangor and Singapore. From 1975 to 1981, the two rivals contested six out of seven finals. Ahead of the first game, Singapore felt that history was on their side after winning in 1955 and 1965.

Before it all kicked off in 1975, the FAS pledged that the team would make it all the way to the final. If a year ending in one is said to be lucky for Tottenham Hotspur, then a year ending in five was said to be lucky for the Lions.

After a 6-0 aggregate semi-final win over Kelantan, that confidence did not seem misplaced, with star player Dollah Kassim scoring nine goals on the road to Kuala Lumpur.

The two teams had met 17 times in the final—an incredible number in the old Malaya Cup—but this was their first meeting in a Malaysia Cup final, as the new trophy had been called since 1967.

Singapore's win in 1965 was still fresh in the mind. Selangor had been 1-0 ahead until the last 15 minutes when the Lions netted three goals.

But there were issues leading up to the 1975 final. Four of Singapore's best players—Dollah Kassim, Lim Teng Sai, S. Rajagopal and M. Kumar—could not get time off work for full-time, centralised training. Others had to return to their jobs after morning training and then return for late afternoon sessions. There were also injury doubts over captain Seak Poh Leong and striker Arshad Khamis.

And then there was Selangor, a team packed full of talent, full of legends of Malaysian football. R. Arumugam, Soh Chin Aun, Wong Choon Wah and, of course, the mighty Mokhtar Dahari, who had been in fine goal-scoring form.

The big day was 31 August 1975, and Singapore just never got going. Dollah Kassim had been on fire but just could not find a way past his old enemy Santokh Singh in the Selangor defence.

In front of over 30,000 fans at the Merdeka, the Red Giants were dominant from the beginning, though "SuperMokh" was not quite as deadly as usual. It fell to Abdullah Ali who fired home from 20 metres, a fierce shot, that had to be, to beat the in-form Eric Paine in the

Singapore goal. At the end, Paine and the skipper, Seak Poh Leong, were in tears.

The mighty Soh Chin Aun was happy, but like the professional he was, the captain wanted more. "I am very happy that we won but what a pity for me because I missed a double. This is the first time I am skipper of both the national team and Selangor. I was hoping for the Merdeka title and the Malaysia Cup title to make it a grand double. I missed it, but I am still happy to have at least one title under my debut captaincy this year."

The same two teams met in the final a year later, with Singapore once again winning their semi-final, this time against Pahang, 6-0.

In the final, Selangor ran out 3-0 winners, even though Singapore's performance was a little better than the one 12 months previously. Some blamed the defeat on the decision to keep the players holed up in a Kuala Lumpur hotel for days before the game, making the players too tense. Another issue was the dramatic recall of goalkeeper Lim Chiew Peng for the first time in 18 months. Eric Paine, so impressive a year earlier, was out.

Selangor were delighted, as their FA president Dato Harun said in words that sound incredibly undiplomatic now: "We need an early goal and Paine could be the biggest frustration. Our forwards may lose heart if they do not get the early goal to destroy Singapore's confidence. But with Chiew Peng there, it is a totally different story."

Trevor Hartley, who was with the Singapore team, said, "I cannot afford to field a half fit man. I believe that Chiew Peng will not let us down. He has shown remarkable form during training, and we must remember that he has the experience." He did acknowledge that Singapore were underdogs, and this was no false modesty from the Englishman.

In the end, the replacement goalkeeper was not to blame for the goals. With 18 minutes remaining the match was goalless, until Mohktar Dahari let fly with a left-footed shot. Soon after John Engkatesu made it two and that was it—though there was still time for SuperMokh to let fly from 20 metres to give Selangor a slightly flattering 3-0 win and a second successive trophy.

Singapore returned to winning ways in 1977 with a 3-2 win over Penang with "Uncle" Choo Seng Quee (much more of him later), but then normal service with Selangor was resumed in 1978 as the two met in the final once again.

Much of the pre-match talk was on whether it was possible for the

Lions to stop Mokhtar Dahari. Many felt the star striker would be easier to deal with after the retirement of midfielder Wong Choon Wah.

Choo may have left his post as coach but publicly told the team not to be affected by the atmosphere that the expected crowd of 40,000 would create. He also told his successor Sebastian Yap to "get a tough tackler and tell him not to give Mokhtar an inch to move. If possible hold Mokhtar by the hand every time he crosses the halfway line." He cited his experience in 1958. "When I coached Malaya in the Merdeka tournament, we met Hong Kong, the defending champions. In that Hong Kong side we faced Yiu Cheuk Yin, Asia's deadliest striker.

"I drew up a plan whereby Malayan skipper Mok Yai Hoon was detailed to mark Cheuk Yin whenever he moved into our half." It worked, as the game ended in a 3-1 win.

Yap did not heed Uncle Choo as Selangor defeated their rivals 4-2. Choo had advised the Reds to slow the game down. That also did not happen.

It started well for the visitors as Hasli Ibrahim headed home in the thirty-third minute. Two minutes later Quah Kim Song's header also evaded goalkeeper Abdul Rashid Hassan who was immediately replaced by the "Spiderman", R. Arumugam. The 10,000 Singapore fans couldn't believe that their team was 2-0 up so early, and neither could the team. Within moments, Ramil Junid scored for Selangor to reduce the arrears.

In the second half, Selangor turned the screw but Singapore held on until 14 minutes from time when Soh Chin Aun lashed home a free-kick. When John Engkatesu put the Red Giants ahead four minutes from time, it was obvious that it was all over, but there was still enough seconds on the clock for Ramli Junit to make it 4-2.

Coach Yap faced calls to resign—he was soon on his way—from angry fans as once again, Selangor demonstrated their superiority.

Inevitably, the two rivals met again in 1979 and once again, the Malaysians took the trophy, winning 2-0. Singapore was as sick at the sight of Selangor as much as Penang had once been sick at the sight of them. The last time Singapore had beaten Selangor in a final had happened way back in 1965.

But then came a new decade, and as Singapore prepared for another final against Selangor in 1980, coach Jita Singh was leaving nothing to chance. He confined his players to their KL hotels. Those who went out were accompanied by FAS officials. "This is war in peacetime," Jita said. "I can't afford to make a slip. The war has started."

As well as a new decade, there was a new hero and a new outcome for Singapore. The Lions won 2-1 at the Merdeka Stadium to send their 4,000 travelling fans wild with delight.

They cared little that the game was not as epic as some past encounters. Singapore took the lead early when Leong Kok Fann converted a Fandi Ahmad cross. The joy was short-lived as, in the nineteenth minute, Mokhtar headed home an equaliser, but the star was nursing a knee injury and was not at his devastating best.

The match became cagey until early in the second half, when Fandi scored what turned out to be the winning goal to silence the home fans and put the Lions on the path to a very welcome and overdue win over their rivals.

Fandi—just turned 18—took the headlines with his match-winning performance and also earned plaudits for coach Jita Singh, who had rested his young star for the previous three cup ties. "He was fit enough…" said the boss, adding, "But I kept him for the final to work up his appetite for goals." On such decisions, reputations can be made or broken. Had Fandi and Singapore failed, then the reaction may have been very different. Interestingly, the forward had been rested for an earlier game with Selangor, so the Malaysians would not get a look at him. They would get plenty more over the next few years.

The players returned home to a mighty welcome. Fandi was lifted into the air by fans as he returned to Paya Lebar Airport the following day. Captain Samad Allapitchay was told by FAS boss N. Ganesan that he had to cancel his plans to step down from the national team. "I'm not appealing to you, but I'm ordering you to stay on."

As it was, the skipper was still there in 1981 when the two teams met in the final for the sixth time in seven years. He must have wished that he had stuck to his original plan. Selangor ran out 4-0 winners but there were allegations of match-fixing.

Karl-Heinz Weigang, a German coach who had been working with Malaysia (and was still coaching Kedah in 2017 not long before he sadly passed away), remarked that Singapore had not done much work. "Skilful Singapore allowed themselves to be totally deprived of activity. They did the minimum amount of running, harassing, tackling and winning the ball and Selangor were made to look very superior…Selangor were literally laughing in the rain at Singapore's lack of resistance!"

Singapore coach Jita Singh claimed the match had been fixed. He said he had been informed before the match that five players were ready to sell the match. "Even if I believed the forewarnings, I couldn't have done anything about it. There was no way I could substitute the five players at the last minute…" He said that he noticed that the five players played their worse game ever. "Their poor performance couldn't be attributed to Cup final jitters." That much is true given the number of finals the team had played in previous years. The coach called for an investigation.

Skipper Samad came out a few days later to deny the claims made by the coach. "I'm very disturbed by the allegations…" he said. "What utter rubbish! What's coach Jita Singh trying to prove? Is he trying to tell the world that Singapore lost because a few players, as he alleges, were on the 'take'? If that's the only reason…then I say Jita's very wrong. We lost for two simple reasons—firstly, Jita chose the wrong tactics; and secondly, our players simply didn't show guts or fighting spirit."

The player added that the coach was "trying to cover up his own failings…I'm captain of the Singapore team, so naturally, my reputation's at stake too."

"I hope the inquiry set up to probe the allegations will clear all the members of the team." He got his wish, as that is what happened. It was, however, a painful way for Singapore to lose a last ever final against Selangor.

This cloud contributed to Singapore not being invited to the next three competitions, but crowd trouble in the 1981 semi-final between the Lions and Johor was also a factor. Johor accused their neighbours of arrogance and threatened to withdraw from the competition if Singapore was not ejected. Some felt that Johor's complaints carried the whiff of sour grapes after being defeated with the final in sight. (Pahang had also made similar demands in 1976 after losing to the Lions at the same stage, but then calls for expulsion were ignored.)

That three-year hiatus led many stars, such as Fandi, to join Malaysian teams. The Lions returned to the fold in 1985 but it was never the same again.

They reached the final in both 1990 and 1993, only to lose both times to Kedah. A 1994 win over Pahang was the last time the trophy went back across the Causeway but the following year, Singapore left the Malaysia Cup with 24 wins, a tally only outranked by Selangor's mighty haul of 33.

But that wasn't the end of Singaporean involvement in Malaysian club football. Not by a long way.

CHAPTER 3

SINGAPORE VERSUS
THE STATES:
LIONSXII IN MALAYSIA

Every time we step onto the pitch, whether for 10 minutes or an entire game, we can feel the rivalry. It's kind of a reunion for us...

—Fandi Ahmad

As an outsider, it was always a little hard for me to get my head around Singapore playing Malaysian states. It surely made sense at one time in their shared history but after the split into the late 20th century, it seemed a little strange—interesting, but strange. Yet as Trevor Hartley said: "There was always a desire to beat the states in Malaysia, to get those regional bragging rights. It was important and these were games that you should not lose as a coach."

A book on its own could be written about the rivalry between Singapore and Selangor, one that had its own trophy with the Sultan of Selangor Cup. This ended in 2009, but was revived in 2017, featuring a selection team from the Malaysian state and something similar from the S-League. Fandi Ahmad (who else?) was in charge of the Singapore side. He said, "It's all about friendship but it's also a match between two main rivals. Every time we step onto the pitch, whether for 10 minutes or an entire game, we can feel the rivalry. It's kind of a reunion for us, but we've got to bring the best players because we want to win it."

The most recent example of competitive action at club level saw the LionsXII of Singapore go and play in the Malaysia Super League (MSL), with the Harimau Muda ("Young Tigers") going the other way to participate in the S-League. The plan included the two teams consisting of Under-23s players, but Singapore's would have five senior stars there to guide the youngsters through the rigours of the Malaysian season.

When the four-season agreement was announced in 2011, it seemed to signal a new era of integration and engagement between the two countries. "There is always a special romance between Singapore and Malaysian football," said then FAS boss Zainudin Nordin. "The key points of this partnership cannot be achieved overnight, but these are positive developments, and it's a win-win situation for both parties."

There was and is some debate about that last point, but it was at least a return to former times. Singapore had last participated in the MSL back in 1994, winning the league and Malaysia Cup double. With the new professional S-League preparing to kick off, Singapore had duties closer to home to consider.

The Malaysian league was originally set up as a qualifying round for the Malaysia Cup, but got its own trophy in 1982. It turned semi-pro in 1989 and then Liga Perdana arrived in 1994 as the country's first fully professional league.

But from 2012 to 2015, the Lions were in tiger territory, and vice-versa. Most of the attention, however, was focused on how the Singapore side was faring in Malaysia.

Harimau Muda did not make the impact in Singapore that their counterparts managed in Malaysia, partly because they were not seen as being that big a deal. The 'A' team did pretty well in its first season, finishing fourth, but in 2013, the 'B' team, with slightly younger players, stepped in to finish second from bottom. Rock bottom was achieved the season after, as happened again in the final 2015 campaign.

The major difference between Harimau Muda and the Lions was that the Malaysians were a younger team. It seems to be a regional habit—especially popular in Malaysia and Singapore—to group young players together as much as possible and get them playing as much as possible.

As a theory, it is an appealing one. It ensures that the youngsters get plenty of playing time against experienced professionals. Fans around the world can point to talented youngsters who just do not get the chances to play that they deserve because there are more experienced stars in front of them and/or the coach is under so much pressure to deliver quick results that he just does not feel ready to trust in youth.

But there is a flip side to this scenario. With these youth teams in Malaysia set up, partly at least, to compensate for the lack of consistent youth development by clubs in the country, they also serve to remove at least some motivation for clubs to try and remedy this. If you spend years developing talented youngsters, then, just when they are ready to start making a difference they are taken away to become part of a national developmental team, you are entitled to ask what is the point of producing and training them in the first place.

There's more. In a normal club scenario, a promising youngster can be brought slowly into the fold rather than tossed into the arena. He then learns the game from experienced professionals. He gets a few minutes off the bench here and there and there is as little pressure as possible placed on his slender shoulders. If things go well, he slowly becomes a valued squad member and then a fully-fledged regular starter.

There were other examples of youth teams in senior leagues. The All India Football Federation (AIFF) created the Indian Arrows in 2010. This was an Under-23 team that played in the country's professional league and was supposed to equip players for the 2018 World Cup. While some fine youngsters did appear for the team, results were not great. The Arrows finished ninth out of 14 teams, but then dropped to 13 and 12. The experiment was ended partly due to sponsorship issues but also because there were concerns that losing many more games than they won could have an effect on the confidence and development of the players. It becomes hard to develop or play a natural game when you are always on the backfoot and desperate just to avoid a fourth defeat in a row. It may be decent experience for goalkeepers and defenders, but it is not going to help creative players express themselves and take the necessary risks. Not all experience is good experience.

It does not matter how talented they are, when they are facing international stars with many more games under their belts then there are going to be times when it all goes wrong. And when it all does go wrong, there is no grizzled old veteran to step forward and assume leadership. The Lions allowed older players to appear alongside the rookies and provide guidance and experience, as well as no shortage of skill. When the going got tough for Harimau Muda—as it started to do quite often—there was nobody to dig the team out of trouble. Then confidence falls as defeat follows defeat.

The story of Welsh great Ryan Giggs backs this up. As a teenage winger starting his career with Manchester United, he appreciated the help and advice of senior professionals like Bryan Robson and Steve Bruce.

"This Sheffield United right-back was kicking me in one game, giving me a few verbals and it affected me a little bit," Giggs recalled to

The Daily Telegraph in 2013. "I said to Robbo: 'That right-back's just said he's going to break my legs.' Robbo said: 'Did he? You come and play centre-midfield. I'm going to play left wing for 10 minutes.' We swapped positions. Robbo soon came back: 'Aye, you're all right now, go back over.' Problem solved! I had this mentality that if Robson was playing we'd never lose. We usually won. He had that authority. He'd tell me when I was not passing enough or dribbling too much. Him and Brucey were brilliant for me."

The Harimau Muda were going up against old pros in Singapore without this kind of leadership, protection and experience. The Harimau Muda gained plenty of experience but the first season apart, they became whipping-boys for the top teams.

LionsXII was a different beast. The progress of the Young Tigers on the other side of the Causeway was not a subject that often penetrated the national football conversation in Malaysia, but this was far from the case in Singapore. In fact, it dominated to an extent that some started to see it as a problem.

With the S-League struggling for exposure and popularity, the move back to having a team competing in Malaysia certainly made plenty of headlines. The Lions were big news. In the local league, fans may find it hard to identify with clubs and those clubs may find it hard to construct their own distinctive identity and engage with local communities, but Singapore got behind the team.

Facing Malaysian opposition in the MSL brings something into the equation that does not exist in the S-League: good old-fashioned patriotism and national pride. If the average football fan finds it hard to connect with the S-League then playing against Malaysian states gives everything a focal point. Everything becomes easy—marketing, motivation, media and all the rest. You don't have to explain anything, everyone understands the situation and what is at stake. It makes things nice and simple and it has appeal for even the most casual of fans.

And the Lions relished their chance to play in the league. The debut season in 2012 ended up with second spot and a place in the semi-finals of the Malaysia Cup. In 2013, the senior players drafted in were good ones: Baihakki Khaizan, Shahril Ishak, Isa Halim, Irwan Shah and Fazrul Nawaz. The team meant business and they went on to win the title.

This was a fine achievement, but it was always going to provoke mixed reactions and emotions. Obviously, Malaysians were none too thrilled about the situation. Football Association of Malaysia (FAM) general secretary Hamidin Amin told *The Straits Times* that it was embarrassing for football in the country.

"The LionsXII have no foreign imports and the majority of their players are below the age of 23. That has made the Malaysian teams look bad," he said. He went on to say that the rules could be changed to make it harder for the new champions to register players that were as old as 28.

"Let's wait for the Malaysia Cup to end and I'll discuss this with the competitions committee then. But, definitely, the LionsXII deserve to be champions. They have worked hard to be the first foreign side to take away the MSL title."

But spare a thought for the official. On just the second day of his new job, he was asked to present his country's league title to a team from Singapore. That could not have been easy.

There were complaints, or if you want to be polite, observations that the artificial pitch at the Lions home stadium at Jalan Besar was a considerable advantage. Such a surface takes time to become accustomed to, even for the best players, and many coaches at the time said that it also helped the speedy style of the home team.

The following year, FAM asked FAS to change the home venue from Jalan Besar, but the national stadium was just too expensive for the organisation. Nobody really enjoyed playing there. It was reminiscent of the eighties in England, when Luton Town and Queen's Park Rangers had plastic pitches (nowhere near the quality of the surface at JB Stadium) and they used to beat the then mighty Liverpool.

Dollah Salleh said pretty much the same. The Pahang boss took his team to the stadium and lost 3-0. "It is fine to have home advantage," he said. "Every team needs to make the most of playing at home but having a different kind of pitch makes a big difference. By the time we have adapted to the surface, the game is over. The ball bounces differently to a grass pitch and it moves along the surface differently. It takes time to understand this and adapt. As the Lions players played and trained on it week in and week out then, of course, it made a huge difference."

He did not say that the team were undeserving champs, but that without the artificial turf it would have been a bigger mountain to climb. "In terms of talent, there was not much difference between the Lions and the young Malaysian players but what they did have was the mental strength to come back from difficult positions. That was the impressive thing, but I think compared to Harimau Muda they benefitted from having some senior players alongside them."

If the reaction to the title win in Malaysia was understandably mixed, in Singapore fans were delighted.

The trophy was clinched with a 4-0 win over Felda United on 2 July 2013, the penultimate game of the season and a tenth win in eleven games on home ground. No wonder everyone called the stadium a fortress.

There were major celebrations among fans in the city state. It came just a few months after Singapore had won the AFF Suzuki Cup and it had everyone feeling very good indeed.

In fact, it was compared to the national team's success in the AFF competition. Quite a few players were members of both teams. Captain Shahril Ishak was asked to compare the two triumphs and choose the one that meant the most.

"I think this one," he told *The New Paper*. "This is the one that people will talk about for a long time. It's also my first league title and it is something I will cherish forever."

Future Singapore skipper Hariss Harun was also over the moon.

"I can't describe what I'm feeling right now ... I'm really over-whelmed," said the 22-year-old. "I played a more important role in this league campaign than in the Suzuki Cup, so it means more to me. Plus competing in a league is physically and mentally tiring ... and no one expected us to be where we are today. You saw for yourself, how the fans came out to support us."

Prime Minister Lee Hsien Loong was in the stadium too, with a huge smile on his face. It was a triumph for the whole country, though it is a little more complicated than that. It felt just a little too important. When players are describing winning a foreign league as a bigger thrill than an international tournament when representing their country, then there is some cause for concern. When the country's domestic league is not even mentioned, not part of the conversation, then that concern becomes a genuine worry. With the S-League ongoing, much of the country's football attention was elsewhere. Malaysia may not be very foreign as far as Singapore is concerned.

Daniel Bennett was less than impressed about the whole situation. "LionsXII was a disaster for football in Singapore and we should never have gone. It disrupted our league and it is easier to destroy something than repair it and we are still trying to repair it now. We should have been focusing on the S-League rather than putting together an elite team to play in a foreign league. We are still paying the price for doing that."

Steve Darby, who had coached Home United in the S-League and played against the LionsXII as the boss of Kelantan, was also not a fan of the arrangement.

"It didn't work for a number of reasons," he said. "There was too much attention and interest in Singapore in just one team that was playing in another league. This took the spotlight away from the S-League in terms of attention, media, fans and even sponsorship.

"It also weakens the S-League, as the best players are playing in another league. In the short-term, this may benefit those players involved as they are playing in a more competitive league and that can help the national team, but what happens further down the line? The damage it can do to the S-League will more than cancel out any benefits for the Lions. And then you have the situation that there is little point for S-League clubs to develop young talent when they are then taken away to play in a different league. What is the benefit for the clubs?"

Attendances in the S-League continued to be fairly dismal when the Lions were in Malaysia, but that does not mean there was a clear correlation. What is certain, however, is that there was a lot more written about the Lions than any other S-League team. And the average attendance of around 6,000 was far superior to any other team.

Look through the old newspaper clippings now and there is more coverage dedicated to how fans celebrated the win in the days following the triumph—making replica trophies or printing banners and t-shirts—than there are articles that covered a whole round of domestic games.

The Lions became a second national team—you could see plenty of national team shirts in the crowd—and a great one at that, because they were playing Malaysian teams every week. Not only were they playing, but they were winning, too. As much as it excited fans at home, it annoyed supporters in Malaysia to see their teams beaten by one from Singapore.

It did not go unnoticed in Malaysia that there were 12 LionsXII players in the Singapore squad when they won the 2012 AFF Suzuki Cup. No fan in the world would be happy upon hearing a stat like that. The Malaysian league was helping the Singapore national team outperform the Malaysian national team.

The Lions benefited the Malaysian Super League in terms of profile and commercial appeal and even strength in depth. Foreign players enjoyed a new challenge. "It was good to play the Lions," said Zesh Rehman, an English-born Pakistani international, who spent almost two seasons with Pahang. "They were a good team, and were mentally very competitive, always giving their all against Malaysian teams. They added an extra dimension and it was always good to go and play in Singapore."

But that did not turn out to be enough.

One wonders if Harimau Muda had been more successful, or been allowed to have a few older players to help the youngsters, whether it would have been better all-round. That is not certain, however, and given the history and comparative sizes of the two leagues, there was always going to be a greater desire in Singapore to win the Malaysian league, a competition that they had won 17 years earlier, than the other way round.

As Darby said, it was just too hard to find a balance. How do you send a team to do well without weakening other clubs? How do you maintain interest in a domestic league when everyone is focused on how a Singapore team is beating the best in Malaysia? How to tempt fans to attend matches in the S-League when the Jalan Besar stadium is jumping when the Lions play—and they almost always win? People who watched the Lions when they took the title said that in recent times, the only comparable atmosphere in the country came during the famous 5-3 win over Malaysia in qualification for the 2014 World Cup.

The S-League couldn't compete with such excitement and passion and ended up looking drab, dull and unimportant in comparison.

And it wasn't just on the league table where the LionsXII feasted. In May 2015, they went north to win the FA Cup, with a 3-1 win over Kelantan in front of 90,000 fans at the Bukit Jalil stadium in Kuala Lumpur.

The visiting fans were outnumbered more than ten to one but their team did them proud. It was the kind of big-game experience that is not only absent from Singapore, but is absent from the vast majority of countries in the world. No wonder that both fans and players were loving it. There was still the uncomfortable feeling in the back of the minds of many, amplified by the words of the likes of Darby, that this was not doing the S-League any favours, but there was too much enjoyment to be had. The hangover, if it came, was for the future.

By the time the Lions added the 2015 FA Cup to their earlier league success, there were already rumours that the agreement would not be extended into 2016 and beyond.

And that is what happened in November 2015. All 12 members of the FAM executive committee "unanimously voted against renewing the club's stay in MSL" in a three-hour meeting in Kuala Lumpur. According to those who were there, Kevin Ramalingam, the CEO of Football Malaysia Limited Liability Partnership (FMLLP)—the body that manages the Malaysia Super League, Premier League, Malaysian Cup and FA Cup—argued articulately and passionately for sending the Lions back across the Causeway.

He started off by acknowledging the contribution that Singapore had made to the league.

"Yes, there is a strong belief among the Malaysian teams that a Malaysian-only league is sufficient. But it does help having Singapore there. It means having more eyeballs on our league and another country's population looking into our games and our results. It's got its pros and cons and we have to weigh all options before we can say that's a good or bad deal."

A little later he confirmed what he thought was the right move. "It has been a period of very tough decisions on the way forward for Malaysia football. The disbanding of Harimau Muda will see the injection of talented youngsters back into our league as well, and I hope to see the LionsXII players back into the S-League fold. We want our football to progress alongside our neighbours as well."

"In the past four years, it has been a great period for the LionsXII," said Ramalingam. "We hope the old rivalry between Singapore and Malaysia football will be redeveloped, as it has always drawn the most interest. But the fact is that it was not a Singapore (national) team ... that didn't quite ignite the flame."

Some would disagree, as it seemed that this was becoming a version of the Singapore national team, and that made their success harder to take. It should be remembered that seventeen years after Singapore had left the Malaysian league, fans there had grown unaccustomed to foreign teams playing in their league and Singapore had always been the only one. S-League fans, however, have seen, and continue to see, teams from Japan, China, Korea and Brunei competing in their tournament. Malaysia's situation is the more common.

There were other issues too. With the weakened ringgit, trips to Singapore were becoming more expensive. FAS did not want, apparently, to help out.

"We took into account the cost of our teams going there because of the exchange rate. We asked them (LionsXII) to cover this and vice versa when they travel here, but FA of Singapore (FAS) could not commit to this," said FAM deputy president Datuk Seri Afandi Hamzah. "The response from local teams was not encouraging either.

"Also, I've been speaking to the teams and Singapore is a massive cost for them in terms of an away game due to the exchange rate. We've got to find some common ground and find a way to overcome these things to ensure the Malaysian teams are not overly burdened with an away trip.

"A team like Terengganu, for example, this year played LionsXII in Singapore once in the FA Cup, once in the league and again in the Malaysia Cup. The teams say an away game in Singapore costs between three and five times a normal away game in Malaysia. Terengganu could pay for 15 local away games for the price of the three games they played in Singapore. It's a massive cost. So we have to look at how we can help the Malaysian teams and we hope the FAS will work with us when it comes to these things."

Hotels seemed a bit of a red herring. If the desire from the Malaysian side was really there, a solution could have been found. Staying across the border in Johor and making the short journey across the Causeway as thousands of people—including Singaporean footballers—do every day was also an option that did not seem to be explored too much.

There were also issues about television revenue but overall, these were things that could have been sorted out if the will had been there to do so. In the end Malaysia pulled the plug. In Singapore, the reaction was split between disappointment and a fairly unconvincing attitude of "who needs Malaysia anyway?"

It was summed up well by a letter that appeared in *The Straits Times* written by Melvin Tan.

"It speaks volumes of the level of professionalism that the FAM chose to announce the decision to the media without first informing the FAS. The decision is badly timed and surely the FAM could have been more sensitive and reasonable. As a Singaporean, I disagree with reports which have attempted to sensationalize the decision as one in which the LionsXII have been kicked out or expelled from the Malaysia Super League.

"There is no basis for anyone to suggest that the LionsXII have been expelled from the Malaysian tournaments. The fact is that one party decided not to renew the agreement and, hence, both sides simply have to move on. However, this latest development presents a good opportunity for us to rebuild the S-League. The LionsXII project has shown that local fans will support a good product if it is well marketed.

"The likes of Khairul Amri and Faris Ramli have attracted a large fan base, and it is now up to the S-League to leverage their appeal to win fans across the country. I was happy to read from Khairul's Instagram post that the FAS spoke to him on the day of the announcement and that it is in discussions with other players ..."

Thoughts quickly turned to practicalities. There were concerns shared by everyone as to what would happen to the players who were now without a club. The FAS decided to disband the team and not field it in the S-League—an understandable decision for many reasons, but especially because with the Young Lions already there, it would have been illegal under FIFA rules to have two teams in the same league from one organisation.

Though FAS guaranteed that all players would find new clubs, there were worries that it would not be quite as easy as that.

LionsXII winger Gabriel Quak was happy to get offers early. "I am glad to have received offers from a few clubs," the 25-year-old told Channel News Asia. "But my worry is for those teammates of mine who may not be able to find clubs to join. It was a pleasure playing with them these past few years, and I hope they will get their futures sorted out, either on their own, or with help from the FAS. It's sad of course, but the players have done their part, serving the team well. What we can do now is to look forward. But hopefully we can use what we learnt from our experience in the Malaysian League and apply it to the S-League—because after all, it is our league."

It ended a little sadly, but it was always going to end at some point. The arrangement was a bit one-sided for it to work in the long-term, as Bennett pointed out, "Malaysia never needed Singapore and that was made clear by the way in which they released the team. They have plenty of teams and didn't need us. We have to take care of ourselves and should never have been in that position."

CHAPTER 4

BIG GAMES OF
THE 20TH CENTURY

It was the referee who won the match for Singapore. We were robbed
of victory.

—Datuk Abu Bakar Daud, Malaysian team manager, 1977

While it was the state sides that developed the first rivalries with
Singapore, after independence from the United Kingdom, Malaysia (or
at the very beginning, Malaya) were soon getting it on with Singapore
in games that became bigger and bigger as the years rolled by.

MARCH 1958, KUALA LUMPUR:
FEDERATION OF MALAYA 5-2 SINGAPORE

The Merdeka Stadium has a historic feel to it now but it had not been
long-built for this clash between the newly-independent Federation of
Malaya and Singapore, which was still a British colony at the time. The
Federation coach was, in fact, Singaporean.

Choo Seng Quee played a major part in the football history of
both nations. He went on to become the national team coach of both
Singapore and Indonesia and is widely known as "Uncle Choo". He was
happy to have Rahim Omar available for this clash as, as mentioned
earlier, the attacker had been in demand in Europe.

Like Choo, Omar was appearing for Malaya against his native
Singapore, but if there were any conflicting loyalties, they were not
enough to prevent the pair from orchestrating a 5-2 win over their
home colony.

There were over 5,000 fans in the new stadium and they contributed
over $5,000 to Malaya's Asian Games fund. They were rewarded for

their good deeds by a fine result, even if the convincing home win looked unlikely in the early stages.

Singapore started well, with Arthur Koh putting the visitors ahead after just five minutes. Rahim equalised from the spot less than ten minutes later as Kong Leong was tripped inside the area, but midway through the half Singapore were back in front thanks to another fine goal from Koh. Malaya started to sort out their defence and cut off the supply to the Singapore strikers. At the same time, they began to gain control in the middle of the field.

There was time in the first half for Abdul Ghani to equalise and the same player put Malaya in front just five minutes after the restart. Two goals just after the hour from Rahim completed his hat-trick and a convincing win for Malaya.

"We started slowly but after settling down, we controlled the game," said Choo. "There is no time to sit back however, there is still work to do."

He was not wrong. Amazingly, the two teams played again on the very next day, with Malaya running out 3-1 winners. It is unimaginable today to play back-to-back clashes, especially in the heat and humidity of Kuala Lumpur, but things were different back then.

So was the result 14 years later, as Singapore began to flex its muscles in this fixture.

NOVEMBER 1972, SAIGON:
MALAYSIA 1-3 SINGAPORE

This marked Singapore's first win in five years over their rivals and though Malaysian fans can, and did, point to the fact that this was an understrength team that was preparing to play in the Vietnam Independence Cup in Saigon, a win is a win. But then the Singapore team was also very much an experimental team. What makes this match noteworthy is that Singapore defeated Malaysia.

Both made the journey north to South Vietnam, a country still convulsed by war. American troops were still in the southern city in considerable numbers, though the situation was becoming increasingly grim and soon after, the GI Joes would all be gone and Vietnam would be united under a communist government.

That was unlikely to have been on the mind of Michael Walker. The former Nottingham Forest defender had been hired by Singapore earlier in the year to lead the national team and help build up the entire football pyramid over the course of his two-year contract. Upon the Englishman's arrival, he warned fans that there was a lot of hard work ahead. "This should not take long with proper tactical coaching. Once this phase is over, the team will play to win matches—how to get goals and defend at the same time."

This had not been easy for Singapore teams in the previous years and he pointed out three areas where the country had to improve in order to become more successful on the international stage: nurture the grassroots, find the best and most dedicated players and have the best administration possible. "They are a must if your soccer is to go up. Nothing is impossible if they are met."

He also said that Singapore football had to find its own identity and not look to replicate the styles of other nations. "Asian players have a natural flair for skilful ball play, speed and a few tricks. These must not be discarded for some other country's inherited skills."

Hearing such talk now, it is apparent that despite all the changes, nothing has changed much. Or at least, football people still talk in the same way, and modern fans have heard it all before and are entitled to treat it a little cynically. Back in 1972, however, this seemed to be a new concept, a new way of thinking. Walker wanted to combine the best of Singapore skill with the best of modern tactics to fuse a new style.

"What I expect from the players is 100 percent dedication, and their willingness to learn...I will be firm and this will of course hurt officials, clubs and some employers. No great things are achieved without pain and dedication, and soccer is no exception."

Of course, the problem for Walker was that players were not professional. In the words of one columnist who was looking forward to the Englishman's arrival, the players would be told over the coming months that if they wanted to train and go travelling with the national team then sooner or later, and probably sooner, they would be asked: "Do you want your job or your football?" A tough question for players and Singapore football in general and one that makes the exploits of players from both countries, until the relatively recent onset of professionalism, all the more impressive.

The competition in Vietnam was an early opportunity for Walker to see what raw materials he had at his disposal. A number of players who had impressed in recent trips to South Korea and Hong Kong made way for some new talent.

"There will be a consistent change of players in the effort to get the best team out," said Walker before the trip north. "Players who show promise will be given the opportunity to make the grade."

Singapore had been looking good in the lead-up, performing well and beating a Hong Kong team in Hong Kong that had expected to win easily in front of its own fans. One newspaper there predicted an 8-0 victory to the hosts and were left with egg *foo yung* on their face by the Lions.

By the time they had left Hong Kong, Walker had been offered a job by a club there. It was one he rejected. "The Singapore team is too good a side to leave. Within a short space of time they have shown tremendous power to absorb. It is a pleasure to teach and work with the players. The offer does not attract me. My responsibility is to Singapore." Two Singapore players were also offered contracts in Hong Kong but, like the coach, said no. "We are not ready for a professional career," said one in an echo of a bygone era that is hard to imagine deep into the 21st century.

It did show that progress was being made, and the same was true in the game against Malaysia. After 90 minutes the two teams were level at 1-1, with Dollah Kassim getting the goal for Singapore. Kadir Suleiman then popped up in extra-time to put the Lions ahead; then, with Malaysia chasing the game, Yunos Baba got the goal that sealed the win. Both players were making their debuts.

Malaysia manager Colonel R.J. Minjoot was left to rue his team's mistakes. "It was unfortunate that it had to end this way. The team played hard in all the matches but foolish errors cost us the title."

JUNE 1976, OLYMPIC QUALIFIERS: MALAYSIA 6-0 SINGAPORE

This result is better remembered on one side of the Causeway than the other, for obvious reasons. The game took place in Jakarta and the Indonesian capital remains the scene of Singapore's heaviest ever defeat at the hands of their neighbours.

Yet this really was a flattering scoreline and it was a real contest until after the hour mark. Dolllah Kassim had missed first-half chances that could have pushed the game in a very different direction.

The second-half introduction of Soh Chin Aun changed the game. The sight of their inspirational leader, even one that was not fully fit, coming off the bench, lifted the Malaysians. Even so, the deadlock was broken by a Hasli Ibrahim own goal midway through the second half. After that, the floodgates opened. Mokhtar Dahari completed the thrashing just before the final whistle.

At the time, the Malaysian team, which had previously qualified for the 1972 Olympics, was to go on to qualify for the 1980 competition, too. Unfortunately, the Malaysian government ordered its athletes to stay home and not travel to the Moscow Games in protest at the Soviet Union's recent invasion of Afghanistan. The players were not happy, as the legendary Soh Chin Aun reported: "We were crushed and many of us were in tears. We felt sports and politics should be separate."

As an attempt at consolation, Football Association of Malaysia organised a world tour for its stars, but it just was not the same. It would have been the ideal platform for some of the old guard, who had served Malaysian football so well, to say goodbye to the national team.

"Unlike today where sportsmen are paid handsomely, in those days we were not paid much. Sometimes we got an allowance of RM5 or RM50. Or, there were times when we won a match and got RM100. But we played with our soul, it was not about the money," former forward James Wong recently recalled to the *Rakyat Post*. He was one of the deadliest strikers that Southeast Asia has ever produced and the first Sabahan to play for Malaysia.

"We didn't have good facilities to train, but I guess, it was determination and the collaboration as a team that made us good footballers. Plus, we too, like in the movie, refused to give up," he added.

The movie in question is *Ola Bola*, which was released in 2016. It was based on the qualification campaign and did very well in movie theatres up and down the country, suggesting that it is not only the players who feel nostalgic for the good old days.

Not all days were good, however, and very soon, Singapore were going to cook up a dish of revenge in what was the hottest clash between the two rivals to date.

MARCH 1977, WORLD CUP QUALIFICATION: SINGAPORE 1-0 MALAYSIA

This was the biggest game yet by far, a first ever meeting between the two rivals in qualification for the World Cup. As well as regional bragging rights at stake, there was the vague shadow of the 1978 Argentina World

Cup and meetings with Brazil, Netherlands and Italy on the horizon.

Trevor Hartley was in Singapore for this one and watched as it all unfolded. He had arrived in the previous year and was enjoying every minute of it.

"Allen Wade, the FA's Director of Football, recommended me to come to Singapore," he said. "I went there in January 1976 to run a course and see if they liked me, really. I went home for a bit and came out again in March.

"I was like a director of coaching, though Technical Advisor was my official title and later I actually became Director of Coaching. I was there under Dick Pates, the chairman before Ganesan, who soon took over. [N. Ganesan led the FAS from 1974 to 1981 and was a major figure in the history of Singapore football, being credited with creating the 'Kallang Roar'. Under his leadership, Singapore games were moved from the Jalan Besar Stadium to the 55,000-capacity National Stadium. He passed away in 2015 at the age of 82.] He said that he wanted to put the money being spent in Singapore to better use."

Hartley recalls a push to develop local players. "I always knew that I was there to do more grassroots work, to run coaching courses and work with the Singapore sports council. Kids got a dollar every Sunday to turn up and play football. It was a good set-up. There was a high level of schooling there.

"The players were amateurs, but there were some good players. They didn't have a professional background. When I first went, I took over the national team and we got to the Malaysia Cup final. Ganny then put Choo Seng Quee as national team coach."

This changed things. The players may not have had a professional background, but despite his nickname of "Uncle Choo", the new coach was not exactly avuncular and he demanded professional levels of dedication to the Singapore cause.

Hartley remembers it well. "People always got angry when Choo was around. The players didn't like some of his training methods, but he didn't care. He was one of the old guard. Actually, he was all of the old guard! Ganesan was worried that Choo may be upsetting me, but it was OK. I was happy. Choo had a habit of upsetting people but he was a good coach."

Choo even managed to upset the Japanese during the war. "Do you know, I was a British agent in 1942 during the Japanese occupation?" he told Joe Dorai of *The Straits Times* in 1978. "I was then the manager of the *Macao Tribune*, which was sponsored by the British. I started writing propaganda for the British without getting caught." He also revealed how he once had to walk back from Macao to China—a journey that took five nights—after smuggling his friend's fiancé in the opposite direction.

As amazing as all of that was, this game was perhaps the finest hour of a fine career for a man who had the unique experience of being the national team coach of not just Malaysia and Singapore but also Indonesia.

Choo played for Singapore in the Malaya Cup, winning it in 1937 and losing the final to Selangor in the following year. He was also a major figure in the Chinese scene, playing for the Malayan Chinese team that appeared in Manila, Hong Kong and Macau in 1939. Choo was expected to represent China in the 1940 Olympics, which has originally been scheduled to take place in Tokyo. However, the Sino-Japanese War (1937–45) meant that the games, which had already been moved to Helsinki, were cancelled.

Choo then became a coach, with the second phase of his career being even more successful than the first. In 1949 he coached Singapore's Malaya Cup team. A year later, he was in charge of Indonesia, taking the Merah Putih to the 1951 Asian Games in India. There, he and his team were unlucky as they were drawn against the hosts in New Delhi. India were strong at the time and had qualified for the 1950 World Cup, though had elected not to go to Brazil after being told they could not play bare-footed.

As we saw earlier, Choo went on to coach the newly-independent Federation of Malaya in 1958, defeating Singapore in his first game in charge and then winning the Merdeka Cup, the second edition of the tournament. Gold followed at the 1961 South East Asian Peninsular (SEAP) Games and a bronze medal in the 1962 Asian Games. His contract came to an end in the following year when he started to coach youth teams in Malaya, in what was a job created for him by prime minister Tunku Abdul Rahman. Finally, he accepted an offer in 1964 from Singapore for just two months. It was long enough to win the Malaya Cup and the Aw Hoe Cup.

In 1965, he was appointed by SAFA to take joint control of the Singapore national team along with Harith Omar with Singapore going on to win the Malaya Cup and the Aw Hoe Cup once again.

Choo then took the team to Kuala Lumpur for the SEAP Games

in December 1965, but it did not end well. At the end of it, the team manager Tan Peng Gee accused the coach and six of his players of gross misbehaviour and insubordination. SAFA's council decided to relieve Choo of his duties after it was revealed that Choo had ignored Tan's instructions and also incited resentment among the players.

In a letter to SAFA, Choo, who was also representing the six players, said "the allegations came as a shock to all of us. I must be given a chance to clear myself." Choo wanted the Singapore Olympic and Sports Council to set up an independent inquiry. It did not happen and Choo left.

He was in charge of the national team in September 1976 after being appointed by Ganesan. By this time, his reputation had been fully restored and his influence from when he became a coach in his forties to his death in 1983 was clear. He was like a tough Arsene Wenger, responsible for advances in nutrition, tactics and psychology as a coach. "He was ahead of his time in many ways," says Hartley. "He knew that there was more to football than just tactics and players, and knew that there were ways to get better performances from the players but in some ways, the knowledge to do it just wasn't widespread enough."

Choo Seng Quee had been in the hotseat for just a few months—and had been welcomed, too—but there had been some misgivings leading up to the qualification campaign. In fact, results had been dreadful. There had been five straight defeats, with Singapore conceding 22 goals and finding the net not once. It ended a dismal 1976 for sports in the country, with the Olympics held in Montreal being entirely forgettable.

Petitions had been handed in to FAS demanding that something be done about the toothless and lifeless Lions, because the fear was that they were about to be slaughtered in qualification. The prospect of an opening game against Thailand didn't sound too bad if you had managed to forget the 6-0 thrashing that the War Elephants had handed out to them in December. But nobody in Singapore had forgotten.

One petition went: "Results are pathetic because Choo's methods are outmoded and because of his poor rapport with players. Players like Arshad and Dollah who showed signs of improvement under Mr. Hartley are now playing like beginners. Time is running short and Seng Quee must be replaced before it is too late for even Mr. Hartley to do anything."

Singapore had also lost 5-0 to Russia's Under-23 team and then lost 3-1 to Brno of Czechoslovakia, followed by a 4-1 loss to Neuchâtel

Xamax. There was also a 4-0 defeat to a South Korea team that had often crossed swords with Malaysia. Korean coach Oh Wan Kon told the Singapore media that their team was not in the same class as Malaysia.

With that in mind, FAS had called for a centralised training regime starting from 1 February, giving the players almost a full month together—though, of course, many of the players still had day jobs and FAS requested that these men be released at 4pm to join the daily training sessions. Morning training had been scrapped in order to give the players some rest. Even those who had been recently married were not to be spared from the set-up and two of the squad, full-back Hasli Ibrahim and Gulam Mohammed, had arranged to get hitched in early February. This was frowned upon by coach Choo, who had called for sacrifices to be made.

The players likened the dormitory lifestyle to prison and complained of being made to lift weights for three hours in the sunshine. There was some serious disquiet and it was all threatening to fall apart. Fortunately, FAS listened and the team moved into a hotel. By the end, coach Choo proclaimed that the players were "300 per cent better in fitness and skills. The team that makes the least mistakes, takes advantage of opportunities given and rises to the occasion will win matches. It'll be survival of the fittest."

It all came together in the opening game. Despite, or perhaps, because of that recent 6-0 beating, Singapore gave everything against Thailand and ran out 2-0 winners. It was a scoreline that slightly flattered the hosts, but after their recent bad run of results nobody cared that the opener from S. Rajagopal came courtesy of a deflected free-kick. Quah Kim Song got the other.

There then followed a 2-2 draw with a talented Hong Kong team. Journalists that had been blasting Choo just weeks before started to pay tribute to his preparations in producing a fit and hungry pack of Lions. Hong Kong had been expected to take the points but had to be content with a draw. They were not happy to be held by Singapore.

The Lions did not dwell on that, as the third game was coming up and that was against Malaysia.

All the games in Group One took place at the National Stadium in Singapore, but this was not something that was going to faze the Tigers. Malaysia still had a number of players who had taken the team to the 1972 Olympic Tournament, such as goalkeeper "Spiderman" R. Arumugam. In front of him in defence were Soh Chin Aun and

Santokh Singh. In midfield, Wong Choon Wah was vital with Abdullah Ali providing penetration and creativity.

They also had Mokhtar Dahari, but not for these games. The menacing marauder with thighs like thunder had undergone surgery and his absence was, obviously, a big blow, but the emergence of James Wong placated the fans. The tall striker had played in Australia and offered an aerial threat and physical power alongside Isa Bakar, who was not long recovered from a motorcycle accident the previous year.

Malaysia arrived in qualification with genuine hopes of making it all the way to Argentina. If Asia had been allocated four spots as today, then it could have been very different, as Malaysia could have mounted a good case for being one of the best four teams on the continent.

Coach M. Kuppan was just 38 during qualification and one of the youngest coaches around. But he had plenty of experience, taking over the team in 1972 after completing a course at Dettmar Cramer's school of coaching. He quickly delivered by taking the team to the final of the 1973 King's Cup and the South Vietnam Independence Day tournaments.

They were certainly favourites to top the preliminary group, which contained not only the hosts but Thailand, Indonesia and Hong Kong, with Sri Lanka withdrawing. While Singapore had been getting thrashed in Bangkok in December, Malaysia had topped their group in the King's Cup and eliminated South Korea on penalties in the semi-finals—and all this with a second string team. They tied the Thais in the final and ended up sharing the trophy. The reigning Merdeka champions were full of confidence and talent.

They had warmed up with friendlies against European opposition. A 2-1 loss against a talented Red Star Belgrade at the Merdeka Stadium in Kuala Lumpur went down very well.

One newspaper noted that, "Seldom in the past has there been so much intelligent movement on and off the ball by a Malaysian team, such a determined and confident show of skills. If Malaysia can reproduce this form in Singapore, there should be little doubt about our ability to qualify for the next round of the World Cup competition."

An opening game against Thailand was a goal fest, with a 6-4 win. Wong scored four. Coach M. Kuppan had cause to be unhappy, however. The Tigers were leading 6-1 and then took their foot off the gas. The Thais hit back to score three late goals. There was some disappointment and frustration as this game was followed by a goalless draw with

Indonesia—but Singapore knew that they were about to be really tested.

"Malaysia had a good team then and we were ready for a very tough game," said Hartley. "But there was excitement around Singapore. Results before the game had been good and I remember that there was a great atmosphere. This was a game that everyone in Singapore football really wanted to win, but we all knew how strong Malaysia were." They had the talent to do just that and Dollah Kassim, Quah Kim Song and S. Rajagopal were good players and in good form.

Despite coach Choo's preparations, despite the fitness of the players and their desire to win, despite the best effort of the home fans who were taking the "Kallang Roar" to new heights, Malaysia were very much the favourites.

They knew, however, that the game would be tough, as Malaysian coach M. Kuppan, who had worked with Choo in the past, remarked the day before. "The strength is in midfield and this gave them the edge against Hong Kong. When we play Singapore tomorrow, we will have to think of ways to break the midfield rhythm. If we are successful then half the battle is won."

Tickets had been sold out days before and that led FAS to allow the game to be shown live on television—and it seemed like the whole country was crowded round sets at home or at cafes and restaurants.

The home fans really played their part. Sixty thousand of them booed every touch of the ball by a Malaysian foot or head. Just after the half hour they cheered like they had never cheered before, as the game saw its only goal.

Yahya Jusoh was adjudged by Japanese referee Toshio Asami to have brought down the impressive Singapore winger Quah Kim Song. Mohammad Noh stepped up, kept his cool and converted the penalty.

Well, he tried to keep his cool but as he said afterwards, it was far from easy to do so.

"When the referee blew for the penalty, I knew it was going to be me taking it," said Noh. "I not only had to score it but I was being watched by 55,000 people in the stadium and many, many more on television. At once my whole body began to shiver. When I picked up the ball to place it on the spot, it was all done by instinct. I don't remember doing it. I heard someone—it must have been one of our players—telling me to be calm. He was encouraging me. But his words were muffled, yet my hands and legs were still shaking.

"So when the referee blew the whistle for me to take the kick, I saw nothing in front of me. I just kicked, and I didn't know whether it was a goal or not. All I heard after that was the crowd shouting. I couldn't tell if the shouting was cheers or jeers. Suddenly I was awakened by my teammates grabbing me and tapping my head. Only then did I realise that I had scored."

It sounds like a scene out of a movie, but the visitors had insisted that the spot kick should never have been given. There was more controversy. Soon after, Yip Chee Keong had equalised for Malaysia. The Japanese official disallowed the goal, however, ruling that there had been a foul in the build-up. Malaysia also felt that a goal should have been given when Singapore goalkeeper Eric Paine rolled over his goal line when saving a shot from Shukor Salleh. The time-wasting of the Lions in the second half did little to placate the anger from the Malaysian side, but much of it was directed at the referee. There were also questions as to why Malaysia did not get a penalty after D. Devendran was fouled in the area with a similar challenge to the one that led to the Singapore penalty.

Unsurprisingly, the visitors were furious, especially Malaysia team manager Abu Bakar Daud. "I am proud with the way my boys played," he said, going on to sound a defiant note for the rest of the tournament and spoke of his desire to meet Singapore for the final qualification play-off. "Do not think that we are out of the running. We will enter the final, and if we meet Singapore, we will beat them. It was the referee who won the match for Singapore. We were robbed of victory."

The Tigers' coach M. Kuppan was succinct: "(Asami) wrecked a national project." He wanted some sanction given to the official. "FIFA should formulate a rule to penalise referees too, with a yellow and red card. If there was such a rule Japanese referee Toshio Asami would have got the red card for the way he handled the match on Sunday."

FAM president Datuk Hamzah Abu Samah also asked why the FAS allowed the referee to be in charge of two Malaysia games. He was reported as saying: "But what still baffles me is why the organisers, the Singapore FA, allowed Asami to referee two crucial matches in a row for Malaysia."

Hamzah realised, however, that there was no point complaining too much. "No matter what such a protest may do to Asami's soccer career, the scoreline will not be changed in our favour." The boss did, however, want Asian qualifiers to be overseen by officials from other continents.

"A referee is only human and will understandably have the interests of his own country at heart. Perhaps Asami unconsciously may not have wanted Malaysia to play Japan in the next round." It is a wild statement, so much so that you half want it to be true. The idea is unimaginable today, that a Japanese referee was so scared at the prospect of his homeland having to play the mighty Malaysia that he, when the chance came, ensured that the possibility of such a game was zero.

Now, as we all know, referees don't usually talk to the press about decisions made on the pitch, but communicate through friends and associates, but Asami supposedly gave his reasons. The disallowed goal was because, so the story went, Isa had pushed Robert Sim when he went up for a header. Asami also said, again reportedly through a "friend", that he was unsure about the "goal that never was" after Malaysia claimed Singapore's goalkeeper had taken the ball over the line.

"From where I was, I was not sure whether Paine had rolled over the line so I had to rely on my linesman." New Zealand official Ron Harries did not signal a goal. If he had, Asami said, it would have been the equaliser.

It took a long time for the anger to subside. Over three weeks later, Datuk Hamzah was re-elected as FAM president and immediately announced that they would approach FIFA about the referee. FAM were less concerned about the penalty but more about the disallowed Yip Chee Keong goal. "We have to abide by the decisions of the referee. The result, as I've said before, cannot be changed but we certainly hope to prevent such unpleasant incidents from occurring."

It was strong stuff, but given that the defeat had blasted a hole in Malaysia's World Cup dreams, it was also understandable. Despite Bakar's proclamations about reaching the final, the loss to Singapore didn't end their hopes. It was the draw with Indonesia and then the draw with Hong Kong that did it. Winning just one of the four games was a huge disappointment for a team that had been dreaming of Argentina. Losing Mokhtar to injury and then his replacement James Wong was also a blow.

Singapore went on to play Hong Kong again for the right to progress to the final round, only to lose 1-0. That was an epic contest with both teams giving their all, with Hong Kong also having to deal with the pre-match sacking of their Dutch coach.

For years following this game, Malaysia had the fire of revenge burning in their breasts when they played Singapore. *The New Nation* wrote in April 1981 ahead of a meeting that, "Every Malaysian player on the park tomorrow will want some kind of revenge or other...if anything, the Malaysians will be out to prove that Japanese referee Toshio Asami was wrong in awarding a penalty... Ask Chin Aun today and he'll still say that Asami was the villain." The publication noted that since that loss, the Tigers had won the gold at the SEA Games and the Merdeka title, and also qualified for the 1980 Moscow Olympics—but they would not forget that 1977 loss for a long, long time.

And what of Choo? A few days later, he announced he was going to leave. "At 63, I feel the job is too demanding and I have to bow out, although it is my first love. My business too needs more attention. My son Robert is at the moment managing it with other members of the family."

Soon after he took Singapore to a first Malaysia Cup win in 12 years. Cars were jam-packed along the Causeway as they attempted to drive to Kuala Lumpur. The Lions had reached the previous two finals but had lost both to Selangor.

Dollah Kassim, born in 1949, was one of the stars of the Singapore team and the vice-captain at a time when being vice-captain actually meant something. He owed a great deal to Choo, as he told Singapore's Oral History Centre. History is perhaps the operative word, as his words paint an era that no longer exists.

"Then every evening we go down to Farrer Park to play so, I think, that's how we love the game so much... The neighbours that I had were all involved in sports. Like George Suppiah was my immediate neighbour, followed by M. Ganesan, the former Chairman of FAS, and of course in front of my house was the great Uncle Choo Seng Quee. So, you can imagine they are all football people. How can I not play football?"

Choo played a major role in Dollah Kassim becoming one of the best players in Singapore's history. The coach's guidance and belief helped the attacker turn his talent into a fantastic career.

One of Choo's finest hours as a coach came in a 3-2 win over Penang with Singapore. It was a hard-fought clash, as games between these two long-time foes almost always were. Penang were ahead at the break and it was not looking good at all. In the second half, Singapore came back to win 3-2. No wonder, then, that it went down in history—at least in Singapore—and the visiting fans at the Merdeka Stadium were singing "Que sera, sera..." as the final whistle approached.

Choo was lauded after his tactical decisions helped to lead the Singapore team to victory. Dollah talked in detail about the game and about Uncle Choo's special influence. He remembers that Singapore were just much fitter than their opponents. But there was something else.

"When we were down 2-0, Uncle Choo took out the Captain, Samad Allapitchay, and S. Rajagopal and they were all good players, you know. In the changing room during half-time he took the band for me, so I was the Captain. I was pretty nervous. When we were in the changing room it was so quiet, nobody dared to open their mouths except him. We were all so worried.

"[That] we could come back from behind, it simply shows that spirit, the mental strength that we had because with Uncle Choo, he's a very good motivator. To him a game is like a war, you know, either you kill that guy or that guy kills you kind of mentality. So, we were all fired up. So, mentally, physically—everything—we were prepared; tactically also we were prepared."

When Singapore then came back from 2-0 down to win 3-2, the feeling was almost indescribable.

"The jubilation from the Singapore crowd was fantastic," said Dollah. "We could hardly move into our hotel in KL. It was so crowded." The players were up all night talking to fans and posing for photos. It was even more intense back home when they arrived at the airport. "I was carried, I was lifted. Then from Paya Lebar Airport straight to Jalan Besar Stadium, we were paraded—wah, unofficial motorcades!"

Singapore went on to make the next four finals, winning just one.

That Malaysia Cup campaign may have been a high point for Choo, indeed 1977 was a great year, but it also brought something much worse. A fall at the Merdeka Stadium led to an infection in his right leg. In September, it was amputated. Choo was undaunted.

"Football taught me many things. To fight and never give up. And thanks to football, it has given me a strong will to live." Even as he lay in bed at the Singapore General Hospital, he was still planning his return to the beautiful game. "I am ever ready to help my country," he said.

He also had advice for a group of players he had worked with just weeks before for the upcoming SEA Games: "Even if I am not in Kuala Lumpur physically, my spirit will be with them. I will be glued to the radio and TV following your matches. Tell them, 'Uncle' wishes them every success. Don't forget what I taught you. You can win the gold.

"To the hot-heads, my advice is never retaliate. When the crowd turn hostile, remember the Malaysia Cup semi-final with Selangor," referring to the febrile atmosphere at the Merdeka Stadium that Singapore had won 2-1. "Concentrate on the game and forget about the crowd."

In 1978, he was chosen as Coach of the Year at the Singapore Sports Awards. He also received a gold medal from the Indonesian government for his services to football in that country. After a short spell in charge of Johor in 1980, that was it for Uncle Choo, and he passed away in June 1983 after suffering from kidney problems. This was a man who had given everything to football, and not only in Singapore.

"He was a great personality," said Hartley. "Everyone had an opinion about him and he always had an opinion about others, but he was a real thinker and was always trying new things, always trying to give his team the extra edge."

"Choo was there in 1977 while I was running courses to coach people who could take over the national team. Sebastian Yap took over and then I followed towards the end. They could make a fantastic atmosphere. But I knew the crowd wanted pleasing, because Choo had pleased them. The style of football we played was based on goals and scoring lots of goals. 0-0 draws did not go down well. Everyone talked about it. You got 60,000 crowds at the national stadium."

Choo helped build all that.

AUGUST 1989, SOUTHEAST ASIAN GAMES FINAL: MALAYSIA 3-1 SINGAPORE

The Southeast Asian Games final is a big deal in these parts. It is especially big when the gold medal match is Malaysia and Singapore. But more than that, this match really is one for the ages as it remains their only final meeting.

This game also brought special emotions for Trevor Hartley. He had been involved in Singapore football from 1976 to 1980 at a number of levels, including national team coach. In 1989, he was given a one-year contract as boss of Malaysia and his remit was as simple as the tenure was short: bring home gold from a tournament that was being held on home soil.

"The rivalry was always fierce and this was highly promoted by the press. Against the Malaysian states, there was always a real desire to win those games. All involved in Singapore want to brag about being the best. The players were amateur and the standard wasn't bad at all.

"About ten years later, Paul Money called me as I had been recommended by people in Singapore football to take the Malaysia job.

It was a great experience and I was there for a year. I just had to change one of two things as they were preparing for the games.

"They wanted to have a younger team. I said that the players are just 26 or 27 and are still good. It will be my decision as to who plays and who goes. That is very important for Malaysia. I said some of these are still the best players.

"It worked out well. The only problem that I had was playing Singapore in the final, especially as the coach was one of my ex-coaches. I wasn't worried that he would know my secrets. I may have let it be known that two players of mine would not be playing in the final before selecting them. I wanted to cause some confusion.

"There was a terrible storm in the first half. We were a goal up and playing well. At half-time, I told the players that they had been by far the better team and that they had to go out and win the game again. I took the wingers off and played down the middle, as they couldn't run with the ball.

"I played one behind the front two and we won 3-1 and it was a deserved win."

The late Borhan Abu Samah scored an unfortunate own goal after just eight minutes, before Fandi Ahmad equalised before half-time. But the Tigers surged ahead with two goals in two minutes from midfielder Lim Teong Kim and Dollah Salleh to send 45,000 fans at the Merdeka Stadium wild.

"The Malaysians were delighted," said Hartley. "I think they made the next day a national holiday though by the time it was announced, it was late in the evening, so people didn't know and I think that many went to work the next morning anyway."

In those days, it seemed like coaching Malaysia was a more straightforward job than it is now.

"I had everything I needed. We used the World Cup qualifiers and then we went on a short tour of Asia to play games. I made certain decisions and used the preparation to look at different styles of play. They didn't care about results at the time and just cared about the SEA Games, so the pressure was minimal at first. It was all about getting ready for the tournament.

"In qualification for the World Cup, we came second to South Korea and that pleased me, because Korea were a very good side. We needed experience and we used that experience and then we were ready for the SEA Games. It really served us well and the only difficulty was against

Thailand in the semi-final, but we came through that.

"Preparation helps. Players got to know me and I got to know them. It is always nice. Managers get the sack quite quickly. If you know you are on a year's contract, you know that you can say what you like and do what you like. The people, they wanted to change to a younger team. I said that is my decision and I wanted to see the older [players]. But you can bring players in too early.

"I was there for a year, and I knew that I was there for a year. I stuck with the senior players as I wasn't going to win the SEA Games by playing youngsters.

"I was still very friendly with a lot of the players and maybe it was difficult for them, too. I felt emotional before, during and after the game, but I was determined. The game in KL, we had a great time until they dipped me into the running track water jump. I was delighted—the only downside was that it was Singapore in the final. I actually was hoping for Indonesia to win the semi-final, but it was a successful year and I was sorry to leave, but I had to go home and join Luton."

AUGUST 1998, AFF TIGER CUP GROUP B: MALAYSIA 0-2 SINGAPORE

Almost all Singapore fans will look back at this year with fond memories, as the Lions clinched their first-ever major international title.

After a disappointing outing in the 1996 Tiger Cup, nobody believed Singapore were capable of advancing out of the group stages, as they were placed alongside hosts Vietnam and the previous edition's runners-up, Malaysia. So as they left Singapore, there was little fanfare and many expected a swift return home for the Lions.

They expected wrong. In the Group B opener Singapore showed that they had not read the script as they matched the Malaysians stride for stride. Rafi Ali played a starring role as he opened the scoring after 17 minutes, while a young Ahmad Latiff doubled the advantage just before the break for Singapore to earn a 2-0 win.

It was a huge disappointment for the Tigers, who had been looking to go one better than the inaugural tournament.

Singapore certainly enjoyed the surprise victory, but there was something else just as important. It gave the Lions the belief that they could match the region's best. Singapore would go on to the final, where they beat Vietnam 1-0 to win the Tiger Cup.

CHAPTER 5

21ST CENTURY INTERNATIONAL MEETINGS

I never would have believed that such a noisy stadium could become so quiet.

—Radojko "Raddy" Avramović,
former Singapore national coach

In the movie *Entrapment*, Sean Connery and Catherine Zeta-Jones are up high in the Kuala Lumpur sky trying to pull off some mega-heist at the Petronas Twin Towers. I have never stayed interested long enough to discover just what they are trying to steal. The film itself was controversial in Malaysia for the way in which the makers spliced the footage of the ultra-modern towers with those from slums in Melaka, two hours' drive away. Politicians in the country, initially delighted that Hollywood was going to show off this modern side of Malaysia, were not at all happy about the image it portrayed to the watching world.

The movie is set on Millennium-eve, a tense time for the planet when everyone was wondering whether the Y2K bug would strike. It seems sillier than the movie looking back, but people were genuinely concerned that as the year went from 1999 to 2000, computers would read this as being the year zero and all go crazy—planes would drop from the sky and the computers in supermarkets would reject new produce as already being past its sell-by date... In the end, just like the movie, nothing of any interest happened.

But there was one accurate part: there were major fireworks all over the world as the clock struck 12 and we all looked forward to a new millennium. But how did fans in Singapore and Malaysia feel about their national teams?

Singapore were obviously feeling good. The Lions were the defending champions of the AFF Championship, defeating Vietnam in the 1998 final. The newly-born S-League was going well and hopes were high looking into the 21st century.

Barry Whitbread, the 1998 title-winning coach, had returned home to England, citing family concerns, and was replaced by Vincent Subramaniam.

Malaysia were still smarting from a disastrous 1998 tournament in which the team collected just one point. It started with a 2-0 loss to Singapore in Hanoi, followed by a goalless draw with Laos that was received, if anything, worse than the loss to their rivals. It would have needed a miracle in the final group game to defeat Vietnam and make it into the last four. And there was no such miracle coming.

Yet the draw for the 2000 tournament offered redemption for Malaysia while giving Singapore another chance to get one over on their rivals.

NOVEMBER 2000, TIGER CUP:
SINGAPORE 0-1 MALAYSIA

The group, based in the Thai city of Songkhla, contained five teams, with Malaysia and Singapore facing each other in the final game. By the time that match came around, Vietnam had pretty much sewn up one of the semi-final spots, leaving just one remaining. Malaysia needed just a point while Singapore had to win.

Singapore had been struggling to find top gear in Thailand, starting with victories over Cambodia and Laos. Six points is six points, but a combined total of four goals scored was not exactly emphatic, especially when compared to the 11 that Vietnam managed against the same opposition.

Then came a 1-0 loss to Vietnam. There were chances against the Golden Stars, but Indra Sahdan and Ahmad Latiff just could not find the net and Vietnam scored with what was, pretty much, their only attack of the game. That goal, from the deadly Le Huynh Duc, blasted a hole in Singapore's dream of a successful title defence.

Malaysia, however, approached the tournament in reasonable shape, despite the disaster of the 1998 edition. Then, the Tigers had failed to win a single point or score a single goal, but preparations for the 2000 tournament had gone reasonably well.

Abdul Rahman Ibrahim got the head coach job after guiding

Terengganu to the Malaysia Cup final earlier that year. The tactician brought in a number of players that would go on to have fine international careers. The likes of Ahmad Shahrul Azhar, Shukor Adan, Rosdi Talib, Hamsani Ahmad and Nizaruddin Yusof can all look back at that time with happiness.

Expectations ahead of the Tiger Cup were not sky high, but it started with a creditable draw with a strong Vietnam team. It was followed by a 5-0 thrashing of Laos and a 3-2 victory over Cambodia that became a lot tenser than it should have been after Malaysia let a three-goal lead slip.

Perhaps it reinforced Malaysia's need for concentration as they went into the big one against Singapore. Abdul Rahman played the build-up nicely, emphasising the importance of the game to his own players while trying to put all the pressure on the opposition. The coach was happy to remind everyone that Malaysia had not triumphed over their old rivals for four long years but then said that the upcoming clash was "the battle of the century".

Singapore were favourites, and not just because they were the defending champions. Vietnam coach Alfred Riedl had played both teams and while Vietnam had beaten the holders and been held by Malaysia, the Austrian, who is incapable of giving anything other than his honest opinion, tipped Singapore to take the three points they needed.

"Singapore played very different compared to their earlier matches against Cambodia and Laos when they played us," he said. "They were physically strong and took on my players man-to-man and were very aggressive. They proved they were true professional footballers in terms of power, strength and aggression."

While he was tipping Singapore, he also warned that it would not be easy: "Remember, I am basing this on just one match of the Lions. Don't forget that they were not too good in their other two games. If they go back to that form then they will be in trouble. As for Malaysia, they can't be a bad side, having already held us to a draw. They are very dangerous on the counterattack. And their two boys up front, Rusdi Suparman and Azman Adnan are fast and direct. They are very effective for their team. For sure, they will play very hard as well because they are so close to the semi-finals. So, it will be a close match."

Riedl was impressed with the Singapore defence but like plenty in the city state, was a little concerned about where the goals would come from. "Your backline is not very skilful, but it is fast and strong and is very difficult to create chances against. I have also been impressed by Rafa Ali, Zulkarnaen Zainal and Nazri Nasir, who plays well behind striker Ahmad Latiff, whom I also think is a good player, despite his lack of goals. It is very important these few players play as they did against Vietnam. If they do, I feel Singapore will win."

There were about 5,000 fans in the Thai city of Songkhla who witnessed a tense match.

The major difference between the two teams was in front of goal. Singapore's strikers were out of form and, according to their coach, there were not enough of them playing in the S-League. Subramaniam said that domestic coaches took the easy option too often and signed strikers from abroad, and with Indra Sahdan injured, Ahmad Latiff unable to locate his shooting boots and Steven Tan lacking consistency, there was a definite lack of firepower.

Even so, most expected the Lions to get the win they needed against a Malaysian team that would go through with just a point. Malaysia could be caught between two stools, not knowing whether to push for the win they didn't need or play tight for the draw that would be enough—always a dangerous tactic.

Singapore had the same problems of not taking their chances once again. From the kick-off they attacked and almost took the lead inside the first few seconds through Ahmad Latiff. It was a committed defensive display from Malaysia right from the very beginning. Almost as if to prove Subramaniam's point, the Tigers seemed to have more teeth going forward—it could have been that playing in a league that (at the time) banned foreign imports helped Malaysian players develop their goal-scoring skills.

This superiority was shown as Azman Adnan came off the bench. Azman was coming to the end of a prolific international career but had already scored two goals earlier in the tournament. The coach felt that if Malaysia could keep Singapore quiet for the first half, then this fresh forward would be a sight to strike fear into the hearts of the Lions.

And so it proved, as he scored the only goal of the game just after the hour. Singapore had already missed a first-half penalty (by Zulkarnaen Zainal), and it was not going to be their day.

"I am speechless," said Rahman after the game, the end of which had seen the players running to celebrate in front of around 2,000 visiting fans located at the corner of the stadium. "I don't know what to say. I am happy that we finally beat Singapore after four long years. We fought hard and got the goal when we needed to do so. We defended as a team and deserved it. Now we can look forward to the semi-finals."

However, that did not go well for the Tigers as they fell 2-0 to hosts Thailand. It was small—perhaps zero—consolation for the defeated team that the Elephants went on to defeat Indonesia comfortably in the final 4-1.

For Singapore, it was a crash down to earth after the joys of 1998. But they would have a chance for revenge two years later.

DECEMBER 2002, TIGER CUP: SINGAPORE 0-4 MALAYSIA

Aleksandar Durić could not believe what was going on. The striker was sat in the National Stadium watching as Malaysia thrashed the Lions. "It was one of those crazy nights in football. It was really bad, with the fans showing that they were not happy.

"Here there is pressure on the coach. If you lose, especially by a big score, then the coach can get sacked. Jan Poulsen was fired soon after. It was all connected to this special feeling in Singapore that you don't lose to Malaysia, and you especially don't lose to Malaysia in a tournament at home."

The clash in 2000 had been a big deal, but then it had taken place in front of just 5,000 in a neutral venue. It was important for all kinds of reasons but it just did not feel like that big of an occasion. Not so in 2002. This was a game that felt big in all aspects.

With 50,000 fans at Singapore's National Stadium in full voice, there was never going to be anything other than a special atmosphere in both games. In the Singapore media, the theme was obvious: revenge for the disappointing loss of two years earlier. With home advantage, this time it would surely be different.

Well, it was, but perhaps not in the way that the Lions had been hoping for. It was a result that still pains or thrills today, and it is certainly still talked about on both sides of the Causeway.

The game in 2002 was directly related to what had happened two years earlier. Jan Poulsen had become Technical Director in 1999 and shifted into the hot-seat, replacing Subramaniam after the 2000 Tiger Cup failure.

There was quite a postmortem into the failed campaign in Thailand.

Going into the competition as champions Singapore may have picked up six points, but those two wins came against Cambodia and Laos—teams that were considerably weaker in 2000 than they are now.

Subramaniam was a coach who divided opinion among fans and was certainly not short of a few himself. In 2003, he claimed that he was a visionary and did not get the credit he deserved. For example, he said that he suggested to FAS in 1999 that a team of talented Under-23s should be allowed to play in the S-League in 2000 in order to prepare for the 2001 SEA Games. The idea was rejected; but then in November 2002 FAS announced it would do just that ahead of the 2003 SEA Games. Subramaniam also wanted to introduce a compulsory fitness test for all S-League players. Again it was turned down at the time, but again it was introduced after he was let go.

"Whatever I have tried to do, I have been turned away at every possible corner," the former boss said to *TODAY* newspaper in 2003. "If all my suggestions were implemented back then, we would not be where we are today, losing 4-0 to Malaysia and struggling to beat Laos. I only wish I had been given the same amount of support which Poulsen has been given over the last couple of years since he came."

There didn't seem to be any love lost between Poulsen and Subramaniam. "It is rather sad because I am not interested in politicking," was Poulsen's reply. "I only want Singapore football to succeed. I have a conscience and I do what I do because I owe it to the public. After all, it is public funds that I am earning. If something is not right, I will certainly say it like it is."

When the Tiger Cup started in 2000, Poulsen was Technical Director and also advising the FAS. Subramaniam was not happy as he felt that his fate as head coach after the tournament had been decided, partly at least, by a foreigner and that this should not have been the case.

"We are both football people. But he has not been able to take constructive criticism, or even ideas from others. I think two cases illustrate who Poulsen is. In January 2001, when Singapore and Thailand drew 1-1 at the National Stadium, Poulsen was quoted as saying that 'the gap between Singapore and Thailand is not that far after all'.

"In August 2001, when the Lions were whacked 5-0 by Thailand, he said that 'the gap is quite obvious'." This was, said Vincent, "quite incredible, I would say, the drastic change within seven months." Singapore football needs, he said, to be able to "take criticism. We have to face up to it if we fail and learn to bounce back. Only then will the fans have respect for what we are trying to achieve."

Speaking in 2017, Poulsen prefers not to talk too much about his predecessor.

"At the 2000 Tiger Cup, the team did not perform so well and Vincent was told that he had to leave and then they asked me to take over," Poulsen said. "There were some issues. The technical director job is a long-term thing but national team coaches work short-term. I knew that could be a problem for me, but I always liked to work on the training field as I had in Denmark for many years."

In response to the claim that Vincent's fate had been decided by a foreigner, Poulsen said that he had not instigated the dismissal of his predecessor but had not tried to save him either.

"The FAS probably asked me about my opinion of the coach and the games at the Tiger Cup. The results were not very good, the team had not played well and people were not happy. They were in doubt as to what to do and I probably agreed that it was the right decision to let him go, so he is probably correct in that sense."

Taking over Singapore ahead of a big tournament did not faze the cool Dane. "I was used to pressure as a coach. When you are out there as a foreigner the pressure is probably a little bigger. Everyone is friendly to you but you are there, taking up one of the other positions that a local could be doing. So I was aware of the expectations but I did not let it get to me.

"Going into the Tiger Cup, we were confident of winning but it was about more than that. About the Goal 2010 project, the government—I think but they never told me—had two reasons for launching the Goal project. As well as the World Cup, it was about nation building. When do you see a Chinese, Malay and Indian hugging? It is on the field only."

Poulsen wanted to get the whole nation behind the national team. "Everyone cheers for the team except when they are playing Liverpool. Liverpool came under Gerard Houllier after winning three trophies in England and Europe. After half an hour, the whole stadium was shouting, 'we want goal, we want goal' whenever Liverpool had possession." We were talking on the phone but I could almost see the Dane shaking his head in amazement. "We wanted to change that."

The best recipe to get fans on board and excited is success.

"Results leading up to the tournament were not bad. We beat New Zealand 3-0 at home. Uruguay were on their way to the World Cup and we lost 2-1 to them, and we beat Malaysia in Malaysia a few months before. I was optimistic, we had done well. I felt we could win and there was no team for us to be scared of."

This was the opening game, and with Thailand already thrashing Laos 5-1, the two rivals knew that defeat would make it very difficult to progress to the semi-finals.

At the old National Stadium, the famous "Kallang Roar" was in full effect until the half hour when Akmal Rizal opened the scoring for Malaysia. Indra Putra Mahayuddin grabbed a second half brace and then the 4-0 rout was completed by Nizaruddin Yusof. Singapore had won the 1998 tournament but then had been knocked out in the group stage in 2000 after a defeat at the hands of Malaysia. Now, to suffer the same fate in 2002, was all too much.

Long before the final whistle, home fans had first started to rip up their red "Roar, Lions!" T-shirts on the terraces; then they started to leave the stadium with the understandable desire to find something better to do than watch the Lions get mauled at home by their biggest rivals in such an important game.

"Obviously the players and I are very disappointed. This was an important match, not only for the team but also for football in Singapore," said a stunned Poulsen after the game. "We never really functioned as a team. I cannot recall a match where we have played so poorly as a team. If I had the answer as to why we played so poorly, we would have played differently. We have two more games to go, and it's going to be an uphill task."

Allan Harris was in charge of Malaysia: "To be fair, I didn't think it would be this scoreline," said the Englishman. "I feel sorry for Jan Poulsen who is my friend, but I'm so proud of my boys. We have a fantastic team spirit that will get us through, but I'm not going to go overboard with this win. It's the first step in this tournament and we have two more games to go.

"All I can say is enjoy the good times, because the bad times are always around the corner."

Harris knew this, after a long playing career in England with spells at Chelsea and QPR. He had also been assistant coach to Terry Venables at Barcelona in the mid-eighties, and had a successful spell in the nineties with Egyptian giants Al Ahly SC. Pressure was not an issue for the Englishman. Compared to the expectations at Barcelona and at one of Africa's biggest clubs, Malaysia was not going to be too bad when he arrived in 2000.

"I couldn't see how the press could have had big expectations because if I asked you if Malaysia was a big footballing nation you'd obviously say no," he told ESPN in 2011. "I didn't really have that many problems with the press—I've dealt with them all over the world and it was no different. We had some good results and all I hoped for was that the guys felt like they were getting better."

He left in 2004, lasting longer than most manage in Malaysia, or anywhere else in Southeast Asia. Nobody expected that he would stay so long when he first got a phone call from an agent telling him that there was a job going in Malaysia. "I had never been there before, but my uncle was in the Ghurkhas and had served there. I told him I'd been offered a job and asked what he thought. He told me to go for it and promised I'd love it; he was absolutely right.

"I thought I could give it a try so I went to meet the Malaysian FA and they were very charming. When they showed me where I would be living, I couldn't believe it. It was fabulous. Settling in was made easier by the fact everyone spoke English and drove on the left-hand side of the road. The weather was lovely, too, everything was perfect. At the start I used to go in and ask what the weather forecast was like and was told: 'Allan, you are a typical Englishman, it's going to be 100 degrees every day.'

"The team that I had was a young team. I used to go in with my assistant every Monday to have a board meeting with the Malaysian FA and they'd say: 'These are the offers we've had, where do you want to play?' We went to Singapore, the Maldives, Australia, New Zealand—I could just select where I wanted to go and they financed it. They were young lads and I wanted to give them as much experience as possible, so I thought travelling around was the best thing for them.

"My goal was to try and improve them and I tried to focus on youth, bringing a lot of young boys in to give them the opportunity to gain some valuable experience. They got to travel and play against difficult and better-quality opposition—my aim was to advance them all, which I think we did. I spent a lot of time on coaching, trying to pass on ideas, and felt I built a real bond with the players. After coming from a big club like Barca, taking a national team was interesting."

In 2004, it was time to head home. "Some people suggested I was going to be demoted and that's why I left—but that just wasn't the case. I was always on the same wavelength as the Malaysian FA. I told them well in advance that I would be leaving at the end of my contract and not signing another one. I always believed that it was better to tell the truth. They understood completely."

He may be right for as long as people have memories of that 4-0 win. The Tigers went on to top the group and were looking very good indeed. Then came a 1-0 defeat to Indonesia in Jakarta in the semi-final, with a red-hot Bambang Pamungkas getting the only goal of the game. Had there been a second leg back at the Bukit Jalil stadium, perhaps all would have been different—but there wasn't, and so it wasn't.

Harris's departure was certainly smoother than Poulsen's. The Dane was soon out of a job and he could not blame FAS too much for that. "To lose by such a scoreline with such a performance was just not acceptable."

The fans were angry. One was Arthur Lim who wrote to *TODAY* to express his displeasure. "The media appealed to the fans to bring back the 'Kallang Roar' and we did. Only to be betrayed by a bunch of pretty boys and prima donnas who think they are God's gift to Singapore!" Lim was even angrier with the coach for saying that the players were not used to playing in front of so many fans. "What a load of crap! Hey Jan—would you prefer to be playing in an empty stadium? You will be the only coach in the entire galaxy who wants this! For the amount of money that we're paying him, I think we better take some of it back and give it to the Singaporeans and help boost the economy.

"Does he realise how important a Singapore vs Malaysia match is? I don't think so. I think he is only interested in his next paycheck."

The feeling that the players did not care as much as the fans was seemingly confirmed in the days following the loss, when it was reported that some of the players had been seen having a good time in the Tanjong Pagar-Duxton Hill area near the Amara Hotel where they were staying.

Poulsen said, "I am not aware of this. As far as I know, the players were in their rooms and did not go out." Vice-captain Rafi Ali put it down to the fans' anger after the result. "Some people want to stir up controversy. The players were in their rooms and nobody went out."

Years later, Poulsen can be a little more philosophical about it all now.

"It was a surprise for me to lose 4-0 at home to Malaysia. I had been told many times that the only team you can't lose to is Malaysia so I knew what a big deal it was to lose at home by such a big margin. There is a love-hate relationship there. They were arch-rivals, like Denmark and Sweden or England and Scotland. When they scored to make it 3-0, I turned to my assistant and said, 'Thank you for three good years in Singapore.' I knew how it was and I knew I would be going home soon. I could also hear the fans starting to become angry."

Looking back, perhaps a tactical change was to blame.

"I played this 4-5-1 or 4-4-2 and we played it all the time. We were 1-0 down at half-time and we were not commanding the game as we should in a home match. Then I did something which I have only done once or twice. I changed the formation, so we played with a sweeper and two man-markers."

Bennett has painful memories of that game, one played while he was still playing club football in England. He had just arrived in the Singapore national team set-up and was still finding his way.

"I came back from England to play in the Tiger Cup in 2002 and they were not good memories. I don't think I had the time to settle into the team at the time. Looking back now, it was perhaps a mistake that I played. They had been on a training tour and they had prepared a lot, whereas I had just come back from England and there was little time for me to prepare for the game. That was my first Tiger Cup and my second international game. I didn't really understand how big the game was. It was all new to me. It is not a game that I like to think about too much!"

But it is sometimes hard to forget, as Poulsen points out.

"Everyone was angry. My wife used to say to me, why did I talk to journalists. The press did not understand the whole idea. If the Under-17s team lost they would start shouting, 'How can we reach the 2010 World Cup if we lose?'

"But after losing to Malaysia, we had to carry on. We were back training the next day, even though we all knew that it was going to be tough to qualify and we were all down about the result. But I was happy with how the players responded. After the Malaysia game, we beat Laos and with a little luck we could have beaten Thailand. We drew 1-1 and had we won, we would have qualified and we would have been OK. We had one chance in the second half when we could have stolen the game.

"I don't know why we lost 4-0 to Malaysia. People told me that it was not fair or square, but I don't know. It is too late to start talking about that.

"The press were very angry and called me everything. Allan Harris, the Malaysia coach, came to me and told me not to read the papers and I didn't.

"I stayed half a year more. After the match in December, there was a poll asking whether I should be fired and, of course, people wanted me to go. And it took them some time to call me in and tell me that my time was up as national team coach. They wanted me to stay as Technical Director, but I refused. After what had been written about me and all the discussions it was time to go."

JULY 2011, WORLD CUP QUALIFIER: SINGAPORE 5-3 MALAYSIA

Who could forget the qualifying game for the 2014 World Cup? The rest of the world may not have been paying too much attention but there can't have been many games on the road to Brazil that meant as much to the two teams.

Radojko Avramović laughs when asked about this game, one that will not be forgotten for a very long time by fans in either country.

"I think it was one of the best games that we played in all my years as coach of Singapore," he said. "The supporters loved it because that game had everything you could want in a football game. When I watch it now, I can see that it is a very tough game and it was hard for us, but we came through. It was a victory for our spirit and determination as much as our skill and ability."

It was a World Cup qualifier and not only that, but a two-legged World Cup qualifier. This game was not just about getting to the next stage, but also about beating the other and pushing them off the road to Brazil at the earliest stage possible.

Durić talked of how the media, which was not that interested at other times, started writing about the game. It was the same for Jan Poulsen, as the Dane explained, "Everyone would stop the players and tell them that this was a game that they could not lose. Perhaps even more than winning, nobody wanted to lose. It was like Denmark and Sweden. A must-not-lose game. I smiled when I saw that Malaysia would play Singapore in qualification for the World Cup. I could imagine what it would mean to people and what the atmosphere would be like."

So could everyone. So many times, these games had been regional affairs but, 1977 apart, this was different. This was an official FIFA game.

"The Causeway Derby meant real pressure," recalled Durić. "They were genuine battles and this was the best." Of course, an old warhorse like Durić loved the experience. "It was great. The atmosphere was always intense."

It was a chance for both teams to get to the group stages of World Cup qualification, and to do so at the expense of their biggest rivals would be something special indeed. For Durić, there was a real buzz all over the country. "The first leg was played at Jalan Besar Stadium, which held only 8,000 people, but it sounded like there were 80,000 in the stands that night. I'm telling you, if Singapore had a 150,000-seater stadium, we would have sold it out for that game. The anticipation was through the roof."

There were a few barbs traded before the match. Singapore coach Raddy Avramović said publicly that the Malaysian defence had some issues. This was apparent in a 3-2 loss in Taiwan in the previous round, which did not stop the Tigers progressing on away goals but did reveal some weaknesses.

As someone who has sat through hundreds of press conferences over the years, it is welcome to come across an exchange that was not "we will do our best to win against a good team" and all the rest of the predictable and inane comments that any football fan could write without even attending.

Avramović and his Malaysian opposite number K. Rajagobal helped to hype a game that needed no such encouragement.

Raddy started it all. "We must play an attacking game because Malaysia have shown they can leak goals. They let in two goals from penalties, which shows that their defence can make mistakes and concede such fouls, so we must go and attack them. Of course, they have also showed they are good in attack, and can score from free-kicks, but this is nothing new from what we already know about them. And as long as our players perform to their true potential, and we don't suffer any more injuries, it will be two good games between two good teams."

That got twisted a little in the media and was interpreted as more critical than it actually was. The Malaysian manager hit back. "It's nice to hear that Singapore have a plan for us," Rajagobal said. "We've got a plan, too. Let's see whose works. Look at the age of my players and compare that to the experience that the Singapore team have. There's still so much room for us to improve, so the pressure is very much on Singapore, not on us, when we meet. My boys have nothing to prove."

Raddy was ready with his retort that the Tigers were the ones feeling stress. "Who are the champions of Southeast Asia? I think the pressure is on Malaysia because they want to prove they are worthy of that title and that they did not win it by chance." That must have hurt, a veiled reference, perhaps, that Malaysia had won the regional title just the once, which was insignificant compared to Singapore's successes.

The ball was back in Rajagopal's court and he hit it back without a second thought. "Singapore are confident. Raddy knows my team and he says our defence is weak. Yes, in some matches we made sloppy mistakes and the players have to learn, they have room to improve. Compare that to Singapore who have Hariss Harun, he's 20, the rest of them are experienced defenders."

Things started to get more heated and Rajagopal tossed over another grenade. "The thing you don't realise is that there are five foreign 'naturalised citizens' in the Singapore team. Who has the advantage, who has to perform well?"

Avramović was waiting. "If Rajagobal thinks we are breaking the law, then he is talking rubbish. Who we choose to play is not his problem and maybe he should be concentrating on the selection of his team."

Rajagobal responded: "As a player, some of my best memories are of playing and beating the Singapore team in the Malaysia Cup. At the time, we were just state sides and Singapore was a national team. Now, the Singapore squad has naturalised citizens and an experienced squad, they need to beat us more because of the squad they have compared to my young team."

Avramović dialled it down and had the last word, though was perhaps slightly patronising.

"I don't know (Rajagobal) personally, but I respect him. He has produced a good team and I am happy he got his chance at international level. Pressure should activate that mechanism in yourself to produce more. When there is no pressure, you cannot produce something special. Playing with pressure is life. It is a challenge my players and I must embrace."

So by the time game day dawned, the anticipation was sky high, the atmosphere was electric and the football clichés were out in force. This was a game that meant a great deal, and not just to football fans but to two nations.

Looking back now, Avramović still gets excited.

"These are the games and the atmospheres that you live for. We played against Malaysia often and this is what sums up the rivalry. We showed that we wanted to keep attacking and attacking. When I watch the game now, my first impression is that it was a really tough game—Malaysia and us played often against each other and we knew how each other played. The thing I liked is that we were always trying to score more goals. Too many coaches want to keep the ball and keep possession in their own half, but that is not football."

The first leg was in Singapore and was a frantic affair. "It was mad. We went 1-0 down within the first 30 seconds, which didn't help settle the nerves. What a start," said Avramović. "Malaysia was winning in the first minute and we could not believe it, but by the end of the first half we were 4-1 ahead and in the end, of course, this gave us a great advantage for the second game.

As Rajagobal predicted, Safee Sali was the danger man for Malaysia. He opened the scoring in the first minute, bringing back memories of that 4-0 away win from almost a decade earlier. The home crowd was completely silent as the pocket of visiting supporters went crazy. But the Lions fought back and some people have said that what followed was the best first half ever seen in Singapore. By the break, they were 4-1 ahead and looking very good indeed. Durić, Qiu Li, Fahrudin Mustafić and Shi Jiayi got on the scoresheet.

"It is one of my favourite ever games in my whole career," said Durić. "Malaysia had a good team then and we knew it was going to be really tough. And we hadn't even started when they scored. But we showed our character then. It would have been easy to just freeze and worry about what was going to happen, but we didn't. We just started again and we played really well. Everyone was there and doing their job. In the first half, they couldn't live with us. We were playing so well and we were all giving a hundred percent. At half-time, Raddy told his players to calm down and try to keep a clear head."

This was advice that was also given specifically to Ismail Yunos. It fell on deaf ears as the defender was sent off, following Safiq Rahim, the Malaysian skipper, from the field of play. The first leg ended 5-3 to Singapore. It was quite a game and left both teams hopeful of their chances in the second leg.

"I think it was a really exciting match to watch," said Avramović at the time. "We really wanted to win this game and I think we used more of our head than emotion in the first half. One moment of loss of concentration, however, cost us our advantage. I think all the players gave a hundred percent and you can see that they are really tired after the game. Ninety minutes is over and there's another 90 minutes to go. Malaysia are capable of winning home and away, so I think it'll be another exciting game."

There was still time for some more rancour after what had been a physical and bad-tempered game. Safiq gave his opinion at Changi Airport before getting on a plane back to Kuala Lumpur. "I think they are very reliant on their naturalised players. Singapore are not much of a team without them," said the Malaysian midfielder. "These players are only good at their small stadium. They will not be able to play their game in front of our fans at the National Stadium. We will beat them."

These were fighting words. The issue of naturalisation had been a real theme of the game. The Malaysian fans had unfurled banners before the game that read: "100% Malaysians, NO FOREIGNERS" and "100% PURE MALAYSIAN." Singapore had Durić and Fahrudin Mustafić from Serbia and the Chinese-born Shi Jiayi and Qiu Li.

Durić had heard similar criticisms many times. "We had these discussions and I had read about this in Malaysia, but also in Singapore, too, people were questioning why we needed to do this. I never had a problem, as I was welcomed by the national team, and nobody treated me as a foreign talent. You have to remember that Singapore is a small country."

Raddy also dismissed the barbs. "You cannot compare Singapore with Malaysia as we do not have a huge base to choose from. We also do not have many teams in our league. What is wrong selecting naturalised players to play for Singapore? If they can improve our football, then why not?"

Even now, he says he can't understand the Malaysian thinking behind the comments. "They must find some excuse because they lost. At the end of the day it is about eleven players facing eleven players. It is about the players you select and how you prepare them for the game. If you think that way and this is their excuse, then what about those that watch the English Premier League or La Liga? They are not watching these games in Malaysia?"

Whatever the comments off the pitch, the local media was happy to enjoy the result. *The New Paper* wrote an article calling the foreign-born players "The Pride of Singapore".

There was still the second leg, to be played five days later, and that was not going to be easy. If the atmosphere in Singapore had been electric, that of the Bukit Jalil in front of 90,000 fans was going to be something else.

For Durić it was special. "It was a great occasion. I knew about the rivalry but this was different. This was big and we could see that when we were in Malaysia. Even when we were travelling to the stadium, it was just hard to get there at all. Just on the highway, the fans had left their cars kilometres away from the stadium. They had parked their cars just on the highway and they were walking."

There were plenty of fans waiting for the Singapore players at the stadium to give them some stick. "I had played around the world and I don't think I have experienced an atmosphere like it. It was so loud." The big striker claims that the atmosphere inspired rather than frightened. "We were ready and excited. We had real character in the team. We had a team that was full of leaders. I think the Malaysians underestimated us and the spirit we had."

It was certainly a professional performance from the visitors though they were made to sweat, especially as the hosts opened the scoring ten minutes after the break. There was a little controversy about the Malaysian goal. The Singapore players seemed to stop as they thought the referee had blown for a foul in the box. The Tigers kept on playing and Safee Sali scored.

The home fans became very excited indeed. It was deafening, with 90,000 fans roaring them on in the knowledge that one more goal would have been enough to send them through on the away goals rule. It could have been a very tense time for Singapore and they could have retreated into defence, but it was a testament to the character of the team that they did not do so.

With 18 minutes remaining, the Lions equalised through Shi Jiayi, after good work by Durić—the fact that both were foreign-born players must not have escaped attention—and the energy, optimism and hope just drained out of the hearts and mouths of over 90,000 fans.

"It was a sweet feeling to progress in the competition at the expense of our old rivals," said Durić.

Avramović still loves to talk about it. "I was very happy as a coach because that win was a result of the character of the players in the team. It was the result of the team spirit that we had built over the years. We came back from that early goal in the first game and we fought really hard, but I was more proud of the way we played in the second game.

"The game in Kuala Lumpur showed what this rivalry was all about. There was a fantastic atmosphere but it was very hostile. I loved it but it was the first time that many of my players had experienced that kind of situation. They gave everything. When Malaysia scored, it felt like that people back in Singapore could hear the roar, but we were disciplined and professional. We got the goal and I never would have believed that such a noisy stadium could become so quiet."

NOVEMBER 2012, AFF SUZUKI CUP:
MALAYSIA 0-3 SINGAPORE

This was the last meeting between the two teams with the familiar figure of Radojko Avramović sitting on the Lions bench. Today, he looks back at how it all started in this special corner of Southeast Asia.

"When I became coach of Singapore, I didn't really know how important the games with Malaysia were and how big the rivalry was." That soon changed. "As time passed, I started to realise what it all meant."

In the beginning the man who led the Lions went seeking out the Tigers. "I intentionally wanted to play games against Malaysia as I wanted to see how we would do. I wanted to see their players and how they played. We lost the first few games but then later, we started to get good results and I didn't lose the last five or six games against them."

That was, he said, one of the most satisfying aspects of his time in Singapore—his good record against Malaysia. "Everywhere in the world there are rivals and there are always countries who want to beat each other more than any other team. The good thing is that I really liked those games with Malaysia because everywhere you go, you can feel it. The stadium is packed and the atmosphere is great. When you work in football, that is what you are looking for, and the players want that, too. They want to enjoy these games. As a player, I hated to play in front of just 1,000 people. I prefer full stadiums, whether it is home or away, and we got that against Malaysia; it helped our players and gave us more experience in the bigger atmospheres.

"I remember the first game that was really important for me in Singapore and that was the Tiger Cup final against Indonesia. There were 100,000 people in Jakarta. I said to the players that all they had to do was go out there and play their game, play the way they wanted to play. If they do that then there is nothing that the home fans can do except support their team." Whatever he said, it worked, as Singapore became champions once again.

But going into 2012, Malaysia were the defending champions and were ready to defend their title on home soil. Singapore arrived to play at the Bukit Jalil National Stadium in Kuala Lumpur, the big stadium in the capital that can be seen for miles around, and the arena that they had silenced with such devastating effect the previous year.

It was the opening game of the tournament and eagerly awaited on both sides of the Causeway. In front of a big crowd, it was Shahril Ishak, the captain of the Lions, who did the damage. Just after the half-hour he ran on to Shaiful Esah's through ball and then slipped the ball past Malaysia's number one Khairul Fahmi Che Mat. Six minutes later, he headed Singapore into a lead that they rarely looked like relinquishing. Malaysia tried to get back in the game but struggled to fashion clear chances. In the end, Aleksander Durić came off the bench to head in a third.

"I thought we gave a good account of ourselves. We concentrated well and the players were disciplined and at the end, they really put in a lot of effort to get this result," said Avramović after the game. "It was nice to get a good result like that in our opening game but now we must prepare for our game against Indonesia."

K. Rajagobal was, once again, his opposite number and desperately disappointed with the opening game of the tournament. Malaysia recovered to reach the last four but was defeated by a Thai team that went on to lose 3-2 to Singapore in the final.

Unsurprisingly, Avramović still has fond memories of that game and the tournament. "Our philosophy was always to score as many goals as we could. I always told the players that we have to score in every game we played. And that was our main target, every game—to score a goal. Let's try to score one and then another. And then we can win more than we lose.

"The difference, I think, was the players. Those players were special. The atmosphere was tough around the tournament. We struggled in the Suzuki Cup two years before and there had been talk about completely changing all the players, but for me that was not the way. I picked players not because of how long they had been in the national team but because of their character. In the end, it was the right decision and in the first game of the tournament, it worked and we kept on playing well.

"Of course, against Malaysia it was special and it was the first game in the tournament. But we tried to treat it like any other game and it worked. When we played against Malaysia, the atmosphere was great.

We knew what would happen. The players trusted me and on that basis, we won. It was all about trust between coach and players. I had seen a lot of games of the Malaysia national team and the Malaysian clubs. The clubs had some good players, some really good players. The big question with Malaysia was whether you always saw them in the national team, but I don't really want to get into that—but Malaysia had good players and always will.

"That 3-0 win, it was a really mature Singapore performance. We played a really professional game and I was so happy because I had seen players doing on the pitch during the game the same things we had practiced off the pitch. The selection of the players was really important. We were under pressure. I think we beat Hong Kong but then we started to lose games. My conclusion was that if we continued the same way, then we would lose more than we would win and we would not win a trophy. So we agreed to build a team to win something and called in Fandi to [coach] the Young Lions, and we picked players from that team for years. After the selection, it was a question of preparation, involvement and improvement. That was good to watch and the fans liked to watch us.

"The win showed how far we had come together."

Singapore was to go all the way and win the title for a fourth time.

NOVEMBER 2014, AFF SUZUKI CUP:
SINGAPORE 1-3 MALAYSIA

Singapore started this tournament as champions once again, looking to go for a record fifth title. An opening game defeat at the hands of Thailand, courtesy of a late penalty from Charyl Chappuis, suggested that it would not be easy.

The Lions bounced back to defeat Myanmar 4-2, though it was more tense than it should have been. Singapore raced into a 3-0 lead at the break but conceded twice in quick succession after the restart and could have been in trouble had the White Angels not scored an own goal late in the game.

Malaysia had been held to a goalless draw against Myanmar in the opening game and were denied a point by Thailand as Adisak Kraisorn scored in the final minute to give the War Elephants a 3-2 win.

So going into the final game, Thailand had sealed their spot in the semi-finals, leaving Singapore and Malaysia to fight it out for the second. Singapore needed just a point while Malaysia had to take all three. There were over 48,000 in the National Stadium and they had little idea of the excitement, controversy and heartbreak that was in store.

It took some time to get going, but once it did, it really got going. Malaysia took the lead on the hour thanks to Safee Sali, but the hosts were rewarded for their persistence in attack with a Khairul Amri equaliser with seven minutes remaining, to keep the Lions on course for the last four.

Then, in the final minute, Malaysia was awarded a penalty after a bunch of players went for a cross, failed to meet it, and fell to the ground. At first nobody seemed to notice that Ahmed Abu Bakar Said Al-Kaf of Oman was pointing to the spot. Most players, judging by their body language, were getting ready for a goal kick.

"That penalty killed the game," said Singapore captain Shahril Ishak. "Everyone was—I think [even] the Malaysia guys—looking for a goal kick and when I see the referee blow for a penalty, we were surprised and we were asking how it happened."

Coach Bernd Stange called the decision a "heartbreaker".

To rub salt into the Lions' wounds, as Singapore pushed up in the final seconds searching for a goal, with goalkeeper Hassan Sunny also in the Malaysian area, the visitors broke away and scored a third to make it 3-1.

There are still Internet memes to be found reminding Hassan that he once went walkabout. He takes it with typical good grace. "That is football," he said when I reminded him of it at the 2016 tournament. "You have to accept the defeats as well as the victories."

The referee did not seem to know what was going on (though many Singapore fans would say that had been his general state for the 94 minutes that had just been played out). There were bottles flying around and he needed to be escorted off the pitch by police.

Malaysia coach Dollah Salleh could not keep the smile off his face after the game. "Of course it's a penalty," he responded. "I'm happy with the players, they gave their best and I'm proud they never gave up even though we drew 1-1; then towards the end we managed to get a penalty and that's it."

Even talking to Dollah three years later, his opinion had not changed. "It was a hundred percent a penalty. No doubt about it." Dollah's wife is Singaporean and he had spent time in the country as a child. "We knew it was going to be a tough game and that is exactly what happened. We did what we had to do and came back late in the game."

Dollah added: "It is always nice to beat Singapore, especially in Singapore. They were champions, were playing at home and only needed to draw to go through. We were calm and so professional in our play. The most pleasing thing for me was that we still managed to score again right at the end, despite the pressure. After losing to Singapore on the big occasions in recent years, the victory feeling was very welcome."

There were no major celebrations after that win. "I couldn't sleep. The adrenalin was still flowing and I spent the night walking around the room. I was just too excited." It was the high point for Dollah, who had inflicted significant damage on Singapore as a player, and now in his time as head coach.

The Tigers, who had not impressed in the group stage, went on to the final to be deservedly defeated by Thailand, but they had banished a few bad memories.

TOP: Aleksander Durić with son Massimo
BOTTOM: Football giants, Fandi Ahmad and V. Sundramoorthy

TOP AND FACING PAGE: Old Causeway rivals: Singapore vs Malaysia in October 2016

TOP: Veteran coach, Ong Kim Swee
BOTTOM: Malaysian legend and Pahang boss, Dollah Salleh

CHAPTER 6

THE STARS:
FANDI, SUPERMOKH
AND THE REST

If I don't kick the ball for one day, my foot itches.

—Dollah Kassim

Dollah Salleh can still remember Mokhtar Dahari: "He was really fantastic. There has been nobody in Malaysia like him since. He was so powerful and he could run with the ball so well. He could score goals from 30 metres or just from a metre out. Maybe he was not the most skilful of players but he was utterly beautiful.

"Fandi was totally different. Fandi was the most dangerous player in the 18 yard box that I ever saw. He could hold the ball, could turn and shoot in a second, could keep possession well and bring others into the game."

If you went back in time to the eighties in Singapore and Malaysia and wandered around the streets, sooner or later, then you are going to come across a mention or a sight of Fandi Ahmad or Mokhtar Dahari.

It might be on the radio, television, newspapers or just fans talking about the stars. It is hard to imagine now. The Internet may have been very much in the testing stage, with 24 hour sports channels a thing of the future, but these players just towered above the rest in terms of star power. It is their legacy and curse that promising young players are dubbed "the next Fandi" or "the next SuperMokh" just as they start to show a little promise.

It was one of those coincidences that they were around at the same time. Mokhtar was a little older, but had been tearing up defences in Malaysia since the early seventies. Fandi had burst onto the scene slightly later, but soon made his presence felt.

They played against each other on numerous occasions but also lined up on the same side on one very famous night against a player who was regarded as perhaps the best in the world. Diego Maradona is now thought by some to be the best there has ever been.

These days, fans in Southeast Asia can watch every single game that Lionel Messi and Cristiano Ronaldo play for Barcelona and Real Madrid, as well as World Cup qualifiers and all the rest. Back in January 1982 when Argentina's Boca Juniors arrived to take on a Selangor invitation side, there can't have been many in the sell-out crowd who had ever seen the Argentine play a live game even on television. He was still playing in the Argentina leagues at the time and had famously missed Argentina's 1978 World Cup triumph, deemed too young by chain-smoking coach Cesar Benotti.

When he arrived in Malaysia, it was still a few months before his debut World Cup appearance. All must have heard about him, however. And the flashlights dazzled as he shook hands and exchanged pennants with SuperMokh before kick-off. SuperMokh played for Selangor as a matter of course but his strike partner did not. "We've invited Fandi so that he can partner our prolific striker Mokhtar Dahari," said Selangor Football Association's secretary S. Anthonysamy. Not only that, but former Malaysian skipper Soh Chin Aun was invited, as was Thailand's super striker Piyapong Pue-on. It was the kind of Southeast Asian dream team, or dream attack, that fans these days can only, well, dream of.

Fandi himself could not believe it. "I'm happy to be given the chance to play against Maradona. I've never dreamt that it would happen. I don't really know if I'll be able to combine with Mokhtar, but I'm sure that we'll both try our best."

"I am delighted to play with Fandi," said SuperMokh. "We are going to try and show the kind of talent we have in this region and we are all looking forward to the challenge."

And it was a challenge. These days when the big European teams come to spend their summers in Asia in the hope that local fans will spend their money, the games are little more than training sessions. "Exhibition" is perhaps the kindest way you could describe most of these performances. Not only that, but often there are only a couple of stars that line up alongside young teammates who would be able to walk down the street in Manchester or Munich and not be recognised.

This was different and it was a strong South American team that came to Southeast Asia to play the only way it knows how—hard. And Maradona was not a man to hold back whenever he took to the pitch.

The fans that packed into the Merdeka Stadium got their money's worth and those of us that never saw it can only wish that we somehow had been able to.

Amazingly, Fandi almost upstaged the man who was, at the time, surely the best player on the planet. Boca won 2-1. Maradona made one and scored one, and thrilled the fans with some of his skills. But the goal for the hosts was scored by Fandi. According to reports, the Singapore star "soared like an eagle" to head in a Jamaluddin Norbit corner.

"It was a beautiful feeling," said Fandi. "I was playing against the team of the world's best player and I scored." Every time he received the ball, the crowd chanted his name, and his interplay with Mokhtar was a delight to watch.

"It was a good game," said Maradona. "The atmosphere was special and the quality was good, too. I was impressed with Selangor and their attackers worked hard and are very dangerous."

Boca coach Vladislao Cap was especially taken with Selangor's Singaporean goal scorer. "We are interested in Selangor's number seven player (Fandi)," he said. "He's an intelligent player and a superb striker who can fit into any team." Was it polite talk to the hosts or a genuine expression of interest? We will never know, but we can say for sure that Fandi was top-class that January night and that he was never short of outside interest.

FANDI AHMAD

That was the story of Fandi's early career. He was born in 1962 and made his debut for Singapore FA in 1979. Two years later he was the Singapore Player of the Year after helping his team reach the final of the Malaysia Cup. Then came the game with Boca Juniors and the offers came rolling in. In May, he was invited for a three-week trial with Ajax. According to reports, the (then) three-time European champions had written to the player in 1980 to promise him a trial. There were also offers from Young Boys of Switzerland, a few Malaysian teams and Niac Mitra in Indonesia. He went to Indonesia in 1982 but a subsequent ban on all foreign players in the country forced him to return home.

His farewell game for Niac Mitra against Arsenal in June 1983 was memorable. "I have not yet decided what I will do," Fandi said after the game. "At the moment, I am very pleased with the fantastic response from fans I have come to love. Maybe, things will turn out right for us again."

Fandi scored the opening goal eight minutes before the break in front of a 30,000 full house to send Arsenal on their way to a first ever defeat in Indonesia, despite the fact that the Gunners had sent a strong team, with David O'Leary captaining a side containing legendary goalkeeper Pat Jennings, Graham Rix, Alan Sunderland, Brian Talbot and Kenny Sansom—though it should be pointed out that the English team was playing a third game in six days far from home after a disappointing domestic season that had seen them finish tenth.

But the stories about Europe were constant. In the early eighties, the question of where Fandi would go was Singapore sport's favourite pastime—Malaysia, the United States, Qatar and the Netherlands were all possible destinations. In 1982, there was excitement as Ajax offered a three-week trial.

These days, it would be all played out on Twitter and Facebook. After Indonesia, it came to a head and in May 1983, it was all sorted. In July, the day before Fandi Ahmad left Singapore to fly to the Netherlands to join Groningen, the striker received more than 400 phone calls. There were 50 fans, mostly schoolgirls according to *The Straits Times*, who camped outside his Jalan Eunos home. There were 200 more at Changi Airport waving any piece of paper—including money—for him to sign. "It was terrifying," said Fandi. "It was nice to know that they had come to see me off, but I was really scared."

It was perhaps telling that he was more scared of schoolgirls than leaving his home to go and live thousands of kilometres away. But then his heroes were Johan Cruyff and Kevin Keegan, players who did nothing if not challenge themselves, always demanding the highest standards of themselves and those around them. Still, there was some recognition that in 1983 this was an unusual move for an Asian player, as there was a clause in the contract that allowed the player to return home anytime he liked if he felt homesick.

For all of Singapore—and not just sports fans—this was big news. For Asia, too. Apart from Cha Bum-keun of South Korea, who from 1979 proved to be a major success in the Bundesliga with Eintracht Frankfurt and then Bayer Leverkusen and Japan's Yasuhiko Okudera, who also spent more than a decade in Germany after joining FC Koln in 1977, Asian stars just did not go to the big European leagues. At the time, the Dutch Eredivisie was exactly that. It was just a decade since

Ajax had won the third of their successive European Cup titles and the legendary Johan Cruyff was playing in the league with Feyenoord. There had even been talk of Fandi playing in attack alongside the great man in an international tournament in the summer of 1983. From playing against Maradona to playing with Cruyff, it would have been something to tell the grandkids about.

Singapore newspapers sent their reporters to Groningen to keep tabs on the country's favourite son. As soon as he arrived in the country, there was speculation as to when he would make his debut. Coach Hans Berger said on 30 July 1983 that the time was getting closer.

"We are all dying to watch Fandi, but we will not rush him. He needs time to acclimatize. After all, he's just been fasting." He missed a more prestigious friendly much closer to the start of the season against recent European champions Nottingham Forest due to a thigh injury. The knock came as a consequence of the more intense training methods in the country and the player trying too hard to impress against amateur sides.

In the end, that injury kept him out of action for 10 weeks and it was October 1983 before the striker made his debut. It may have been a long time for fans to wait, but it was worth it. The first competitive game on European soil came against Go Ahead Eagles and the Eredivisie match could barely have gone better for the new boy as he scored two goals. Unsurprisingly, he received a standing ovation.

Then, as would happen now, fans were concerned that the media was placing too much pressure on the shoulders of the Singapore export. One letter to *The Straits Times* in June 1984 instructed the media to leave the player alone and to monitor his progress, rather than turn him into an overnight star. The writer accused the media of "killing" badminton star Wong Shoon Keat and swimmer Soo-tho Kok Mun. The correspondent C.H. Teo ended with: "I certainly hope that in times to come, Fandi will not return to do Niac Mitra colours again but be on the road to Manchester United."

That was perhaps in reference to the headline of two months earlier in the same newspaper. The headline caused many hearts in Singapore to miss a beat: "Fandi to join United". The paper had Manchester United paying S$600,000 for the striker's services. That summer, the English team had already agreed to travel to Singapore to play a friendly against the Dutch side. Fandi would play the first half for his old team and the second for the new. The Asian star had, said the newspaper, been recommended to the head coach by Jesper Olsen. The Danish winger had been due to travel to England to finalise a transfer of his own, but an injury threw a spanner in the works and he had to stay with Ajax Amsterdam a little while longer. Olsen and Fandi had met at Ajax two years earlier as the former had a two-week trial at the famous old club.

"I always dreamed about wearing a United jersey and soon my dream will come true," Fandi was quoted by the newspaper. "I would be a fool to turn down the United offer. When I accepted the Groningen offer, my plan was for the Dutch stint to be a stepping-stone to the rest of Europe. My plan has worked." So had the story's, as many readers forgot to take the date—1 April—into account. Dolly Seah said: "I would not have been surprised if Fandi had really joined United because he's so good." Lee Seng Ghee wanted the address of Groningen so he could send a cable of congratulations to the player.

One caller to the local radio station had already spotted a flaw in the story. "You know why?" she asked. My birthday is on 30 June ... so I knew there was no 31 June, the date the paper said Fandi would play his first game for United." The lack of a byline on the article was another giveaway in such an important story, but for a while Teo Chong Tee, FAS chairman, was thrilled. "My first reaction was jubilation. The thought that a Singapore footballer had broken into English soccer made me so happy. But it appeared too good to be true and after going through the piece again, I knew it was an April Fools' joke." Once again, the transfer date of 31 June was the clear evidence.

It was not just readers who were fooled. National news agency Bernama and Radio TV Malaysia ran the story too. It wasn't until 9.28pm that day that Bernama contacted editors and asked them to destroy the story using the following cable: "PLEASE KILL BERNAMA ITEMS 58, 59 AND 60 SLUGGED FANDI."

It is hard to imagine a newspaper getting away with such a story these days, not least because players don't move around Europe in April anymore with the advent of transfer windows. The Internet enables stories to flow very quickly, but shuts them down within seconds. It is easy to imagine, however, the excitement that fans must have felt upon hearing the "news".

Fandi admitted the next day that it had been good fun: "I found it all very amusing," he said. "In fact, it was hard to stop laughing, though the joke was also on me. It was a great idea. I'm happy that it made a lot of people laugh. I wasn't much of a Manchester United fan before this, but since my name has been 'linked' to theirs, I might as well become a full fan. And it would be really nice if United really made me an offer some day—even if they did so on April Fool's Day again."

That didn't happen, and in the summer Fandi extended his contract with Groningen. However, there had been more false stories in the summer of 1983. Ahead of a pre-season friendly, a Dutch radio station NCRV reported that a homesick Fandi had departed the Land of Oranje to return to the little red dot. The striker had not even been listed in the match-day squad and fans were worried. Then, to the relief of the thousand or so supporters who had turned out for the friendly, Fandi was seen wearing headphones after being rested by head coach Hans Berger.

In the first season, Fandi played 18 full games of the 34. He came on as a sub once and was replaced in three games. So in those 22 appearances, a tally of nine goals was impressive. He also scored in the UEFA Cup against Inter Milan and came on a substitute in Bari, too.

A brace in the final game of the season gave Groningen a 3-1 win over FC Utrecht and was a fine reminder of his talents and helped him earn a new contract. Hans Berger was happy—and honest—about his star from the East: "In the first three months, Fandi failed to impress probably because of his thigh injuries and the new environment. But he subsequently developed into one of our most valuable players. And I think he can improve further and do better with a longer stay in Holland."

The man himself wanted to do just that. "I would like to stay on but I'll have to talk things over with my parents and others. Anyway, I have a few weeks to make a decision. There's no hurry because we have to study the details of the new contract." It was a good one. Newspapers in Singapore reported that his monthly salary would increase from $5,900 a month to $6,700 month. "Fandi will be one of the best-paid players in Holland," said Berger. "Our offer will be hard for Fandi's family to reject."

It was indeed, and on 24 May 1984, the player accepted a new deal for another season.

Even back then, European clubs were looking to try and make the most of their Asian players. A tour of Indonesia and Singapore brought SG$90,000, an impressive figure in 1984. Anchor Beer and Puma also got on board as sponsors. Groningen's chairman Renze de Vries denied that the club was using Fandi to make money. "Fandi is happy and we are too. It shows that he loves us. We have made him feel at home. Fandi's welfare on and off the field has always been our priority."

De Vries tried to convince critics that the summer tour to Southeast Asia was not in anyway done for commercial reasons. "In fact, our current trip is also part of our goodwill gesture for Fandi and his fans. We could easily have gone to Portugal, Spain, France or any other part of Europe. But we wanted Fandi and people in the Far East to be close to each other ... It is not our intention to make Fandi a tool in our financial negotiations or promotion of trade. Fandi is first a footballer, then an ambassador as far as we are concerned."

Whatever the truth, it made sense to make use of Fandi's incredible popularity at home, especially when he had enjoyed such a good season.

There was not quite as much to write back home about in the second season and the striker spent much of it on the substitutes' bench.

At the end of that season he was offered another deal but the Bosman ruling was still a decade away. But he was offered the lowest possible salary that Netherlands football allowed a professional player to be paid. This $15,000 a year deal was merely done to ensure that the club would be entitled to a transfer fee if the player was signed by another club. Had the Bosman rule been in place, the player could have rejected the new contract and signed for another club for nothing.

There was interest from Spanish club Sporting Gijon as well as second tier Dutch clubs but he returned home, the FAS sending him a ticket. But he did not come back to Singapore. Instead he signed for City Hall Sports Club of Kuala Lumpur.

MOKHTAR DAHARI

There was magic in the air that warm Kuala Lumpur night in May 1975. Arsenal defender Terry Mancini could feel it. "I remember the pitch. It was alive with small frogs that jumped all over the place, very strange!" the one-time Irish international said. They were not the only ones jumping. The chants had been heard a million times before, but it was the first time they had reached European ears. Fifty-five thousand— that was the official figure, but those who were there swear it was more—rose to their feet at the Merdeka Stadium to hail their hero: "Super Mokh, Super Mokh, Super Mokh." Arsenal lost 2-0, defeated by the brilliance of Mokhtar Dahari, not knowing that the stocky striker who scored both goals was an Asian legend.

So much so that in 1978, ahead of the 1978 Malaysia Cup final at the Merdeka Stadium between Selangor and Singapore, Football Association of Singapore's Director of Coaching Trevor Hartley warned of the dangers of Mokhtar. The Englishman compared him favourably to Arsenal's star striker Malcolm Macdonald. SuperMokh was better, Hartley said, than SuperMac. "Mokhtar has got more about him than Macdonald," he said. "He's not only stocky but he's an explosive runner with a tremendous shot, and he's deceptively good in the air. There's no doubt in my mind that Mohktar could make the grade in England's football league, and I don't just mean in the Fourth Division. He would even stand out in the First."

Hartley said he had recommended the striker to Ron Greenwood when he was in charge of West Ham. "I thought he played the same sort of game as Mike Channon, who bases his game on powerful running from deep positions. Of course, if he ever went to England, there might be problems with food, environment and so on. All the same, I reckon Mokhtar is the sort of player who would probably be even better with top-class players around him. And unlike a number of English stars, he's no prima donna either. He's always first at training and he gets on well with his colleagues ... much more of a team player than Macdonald, who tends to be a bit too individualist."

This was praise of the highest order, but if any Malaysian player deserved it, Mokhtar did. He scored 120 goals in 167 internationals, though not all were recognised by FIFA; he played almost 400 times for Selangor from 1972 to 1987, scoring almost 200 goals. He was a huge star in Malaysia and respected and feared around the continent at a time when the Tigers competed with and beat the likes of South Korea and Japan. Indeed, in his one hundredth international appearance in 1976, he once again brought a crammed Merdeka to its feet with two goals, including a fine diving header to see off a Japanese team that included Yasuhiko Okudera and Kunishige Kamamoto. "He was excellent," said Okudera, who was soon to head to the Bundesliga to sign for FC Koln. "At times, we did not know how to defend against him. He does not seem to have a weakness."

Off the pitch, he was a perfect ambassador for the game—modest, generous and hard-working—and it is no overstatement to say that an entire nation mourned when he passed away in 1991, aged just 37. Fandi Ahmad attended his funeral.

Born in 1953 as a son of a truck driver, Mokhtar spent his formative football years in KL's working class district of Kampung Pandan. His talent got him into the prestigious Victoria Institution, one with facilities to help a budding star. Playing in a trial match for the junior team of leading club Selangor in the 1971 Burnley Youth Cup, he caught their eye and was recommended for the senior squad at the age of 18. That was in 1972, and he stayed with the same team until 1987. Within weeks of his debut he scored nine goals in the Malaysia Cup tournament and earned a call up to the national team at 19, scoring ten times in his first year.

Stardom may have seemed inevitable but history could have turned out differently. Soon after his national team call up, Mokhtar almost quit the sport after his motorbike was stolen—it being the only way for the player, who then worked as a clerk at PKNS, the Selangor State Development Agency, to get to training and games. There was a national outcry and soon a new set of wheels was donated by a motorbike company. He made his full international debut in the Jakarta Anniversary soccer tournament in 1972 at the age of 19.

With wheels back in place, his career was soon back in top gear and helped by his goals and the talents of teammates. These included midfield dynamo Reduan Abdullah, "The Boss" Soh Chin Aun (unofficially the most capped international player, with 252 appearances) and "Spiderman" Datuk R. Arumugam, a goalkeeper who passed away in a 1988 car crash. The national team embarked on an unprecedented period of success—bronze at the 1974 Asian Games, four Merdeka Cup successes, 1977 and 1979 SEA Games triumphs and qualification for the 1976 and 1980 Asian Cups, as well as the 1972 and 1980 Olympic Games.

The man himself claimed two goals in Malaysia's 3-1 win over Kuwait in the 1973 Merdeka Cup final as among his most memorable. "After a goal down, we pounded hard with a vengeance. And the chance came when the Kuwait goalkeeper, Ahmad Al Tarabulsi, palmed off Wong Choon Wah's shot. And the ball came straight to me. Without hesitation I fired the ball into the net. The second goal was through my heading. I nodded it past the far post."

It wasn't just Asians that failed to deal with SuperMokh. Big names came to KL to be shocked by the hosts' quality. Three years after Bertie Mee's Arsenal were outgunned, England B were forced to watch the wizardry of the mustachioed marksman with the tree trunk thighs (according to his former team doctor, to massage one Mokhtar was like massaging two "normal" players, so big and thick were his muscles) which, had he been born in 1983 instead of 1953, would have been as famous a symbol of the country as the Petronas Twin Towers. Future European Cup winners David Needham and Alan Kennedy were left stumbling in his wake and Joe Corrigan could do little about the rocket of a shot that found the top corner. Manager Bobby Robson was impressed, saying it was one of the best goals he had seen. The game between a Malaysian team that was still made up of amateurs and the English professional stars ended 1-1.

"When we played England B, we thought we would get thrashed," said Reduan Abdullah, who came up through the Selangor and Malaysia ranks with Mokhtar. "These were all good players from England but it turned out differently. It was one of the best games and Mokhtar scored a great goal, he was too good for them to handle. We don't have that kind of player now. He was a complete player and had everything needed to be a good footballer."

Today it is not England B that fans in Malaysia watch at the stadium, it is the English Premier League in their homes, cafes and restaurants. "We never had that on television in those days," said Reduan. "That's the trouble. The younger generations don't know enough about this era, one that made us very proud. They should think about it more. We were successful. We were one of the best teams in Asia and Mohktar was the best player in Asia." Better than Korea and Bundesliga legend Cha Bum-kun? "Yes. The Koreans loved Mokhtar, and every time we went there they were always talking about him."

His reputation grew so much that any young player who emerged in the region and was small but powerful and capable of scoring goals was compared to him. In 1978, Ahmad Sayuti started scoring in Singapore for Toa Payoh United and was quickly labelled "Singapore's Mokhtar Dahari".

"Of course I am nothing compared to Mokhtar," said the Electrolux technician. "That's why I just find it hard to believe that I'm dubbed after him. Mokhtar's style has always been my inspiration, so I can only try and play like him." He never quite lived up to the early billing, though apparently turned down a chance to go to Groningen with Fandi, preferring to work for Electrolux—these were different times.

Whenever Singapore played Selangor, the focus was always on the striker and how to stop him scoring. Ahead of the 1978 Malaysia Cup final, coach Sebastian Yap (who lost his job soon after in June after the Lions lost 8-0 to England at the national stadium when even both English full-backs, Viv Anderson and Alan Kennedy, scored) proudly proclaimed that he had the solution to Singapore's fears. "I have the answer to the Mokhtar problem," he declared. "Selangor rely too much on Mokhtar Dahari. If we can contain him then half the battle is won. Selangor may play him from a deep position but I know how to counter this."

The man himself shrugged those powerful shoulders, used to barging defenders off the ball. "I am not worried," said Mokhtar. "If I am marked really close, my teammates will do the scoring."

They were both right, kind of. Singapore did stop the main man from scoring but that was partly because he played in midfield. This deeper position was not countered by Yap, however, as Mokhtar was the man of the match, pulling the strings for his teammates to score as they ran out 4-2 winners. The visitors were a little fortunate to be 2-1 up with 15 minutes left but the 10,000 visiting fans that were getting ready to celebrate a famous win had to watch as their team fell apart to concede three goals in the final 15 minutes.

In South Korea, the likes of Park Ji-sung followed and then surpassed the likes of Cha Bum-kun—in exploits, if not in talent—but SuperMokh has had no such successor in Malaysia. It is hard not to wonder what would have happened if Mokhtar had gone to Europe. Separating transfer fact and rumour is tough enough today, but trying to do so when looking back over three decades is almost impossible; however, Arsenal and Newcastle, as well as clubs in France, Germany and the Middle East, were all thought to have wanted to sign the striker. What can be said for certain is that he didn't go. Like another regional great Piyapong Pue-on, the Thai star of the eighties still mentioned by every Elephants fan after the national team fails to score, Mokhtar chose to stay home.

"I am sure he would have made it in England if he only had taken the offer from Arsenal," former national teammate and former national team coach Bhaskaran Sathianathan said. "He always had the confidence to take on players and could shoot with both feet. He was fast, had a good touch and a great sense of receiving the ball in good positions in the attacking third. For a person who was not that tall, he was surprisingly good in the air." He was often compared in build and style to Maradona.

Everywhere he went, there was interest. In 1976, Malaysia went to

Iran for the Asian Cup to play Kuwait and China in Group A. Soon after the games, the offers started to flood in from Persia. The amounts were reportedly substantial but the striker turned them down. "I told them that I was not interested," was the simple reason given. Mokhtar had impressed in the 2-0 loss to Kuwait and the 1-1 draw with China. Kuwait was then a major power in the continent and would appear at the 1982 World Cup. The Middle Easterners were also coached by Brazilian Mario Zagalo, who was being paid the princely sum of US$240,000 a year (around US$1 million today). He was also paid $62,500 for each Asian Cup win, while 1978 World Cup qualification would have netted the South American a cool bonus of $125,000.

The problem playing against Kuwait will sound familiar to young Malaysian fans. The team spent just four days training in Kuala Lumpur before jetting out to Tehran. Then they made the 600-km journey to Tabriz on the same day. They just had one light workout before the game with Kuwait and that was it. Kuwait and China had arrived seven days earlier than the Southeast Asians and had more time to acclimatize to the cool climate and the altitude of 1200 metres above sea level. "There we were gasping for breath, trying hard to breathe after a short sprint," said Mokhtar. "They were difficult conditions. And before we knew it, Kuwait had scored both their goals. When we got into our stride in the second half, we had the better of the exchanges, but still found the conditions hard to cope with."

Not all appreciated Mokhtar's talent. The seventies were full of skilful players targeted for rough treatment. "He was a gentleman," recalled Sathianathan. "He seldom got angry in the game when he was always a target of fierce tackles to stop him from receiving the ball."

Reduan remembers many such challenges. "He always got bad tackles because of who he was. People wanted to knock him down and injure him." It was sometimes the same from fans, a small minority of which took delight in any Mokhtar miss and accused him of taking drugs or steroids.

All who knew him dismissed such claims, but at times the rough treatment from fans and opponents had the striker wondering whether it was all worth it. "I just don't know how to play dirty. A dirty and rough player in soccer is my biggest drag."

He already had operations on both knees and recovering from games started to take longer and longer, but the pressure on him to perform stayed strong. "In 1979 he had some bad times when the fans were

The Stars: Fandi, SuperMokh and the Rest

criticising him because he was just coming back from a long injury," said Sathianathan. "The fans wanted more from him and expected more from him, he was struggling and I remember he said that he wanted to quit playing for the country. That lasted a few months, but [he] changed his mind and came back stronger than ever to play for the national team."

He finally hung up his international boots in 1985, but continued to play for Selangor and continued to bang in the goals, announcing his retirement in 1986 after helping Selangor win the Malaysia Cup 6-1. He was asked to play for one more season, and Mokhtar being Mokhtar, he agreed—but the 1987 campaign was his last.

Within four years, he had passed away, as there was one opponent that he couldn't overcome. Diagnosed with motor neurone disease (research suggests that footballers are more susceptible to this affliction), Mokhtar died on 11 July 1991. He is still missed, not only by family and friends, but by football.

"He left a legacy," said Reduan. "The way he played and his discipline off the pitch should be remembered. He was a great player, but he was also a great man."

He was the hero of Zainal Abidin Hassan: "Oh, it was beautiful to play alongside him. It was my dream. He was a genuine striker, seldom lost the ball and had good skill. He was a complete player and that is why people still talk about him. Oh yeah. They do talk too much, but I don't think there has been another player like him in Malaysia."

DOLLAH KASSIM

It was a sad day in 2010 when this legend passed away, and there are plenty of sad stories when it comes to the stars of Singapore and Malaysia.

Dollah was another graduate of the Farrer Park school of hard knocks, and the sport played a major part in his death, too. He was playing in a veteran's match in October 2009, a game between Singapore and Selangor, when at half-time he suffered a heart attack. Incredibly his heart stopped beating for 18 minutes, but he was revived and released from hospital in January. FAS helped to raise money for the former star and his family and there was great sadness a year later, in October 2010, when he passed away at the age of 61.

In between, he had led quite a life and the football part of it owed much to Choo Seng Quee. Uncle Choo discovered the youngster playing football, and seemed afterwards to make it his personal mission to guide Dollah Kassim on to becoming one of the best players that Singapore and Southeast Asia has ever seen.

His heyday was in the seventies. He was the top scorer for Singapore during the 1975 Malaysia Cup, including a goal in the semi-final against Pahang that perhaps he enjoyed the most—it was widely hailed as one of the best goals that the historic competition had ever seen, or would see.

"That was my most memorable goal. Zainal Abidin sent me a through-ball from midfield, a Pahang defender came rushing at me, but with one swerve I beat him. By this time I was already in the six-yard box, but the goal was guarded by three men on the line—goalkeeper Redzuan Shamsuddin, and defenders Jamal Nasir and Ramli Mahmud.

'With another body feint, Jamal slipped and fell down, and Ramli was going the wrong way. With only the goalie to beat, I pushed the ball forward a bit and pretended to kick. The goalie fell for the trick and dived. So it was an open goal for me." The beauty almost compensated for the final loss against Selangor—almost, but not quite.

"The Gelek King"—so-called because of his ability to "dance" through opposition defences with his mesmerising ball control—was there in 1977 as Singapore won the trophy for the first time in 12 years, beating old friends Penang in a thrilling 3-2 final.

It wasn't always plain sailing. Like a number of skilful players in England in the seventies, Dollah had run-ins with football authorities and he was not always able to swerve his way out of trouble. In September 1974, he was kicked off the national team squad for missing training. Apparently Dollah had told the coaching staff that he needed a rest.

"When Dollah skipped the first training on Tuesday night he automatically disqualified himself from the squad," said FAS deputy chairman N. Ganesan. "But we certainly do not want players who give us a multitude of excuses. Tuesday night's excuse was the last straw as far as FAS and Dollah Kassim are concerned. FAS also doesn't want to develop players who get swollen headed or hold us to ransom. We can't dance to their tune."

Strong words, but FAS had been fuming as Dollah had not been named in the original squad but was called up after the player had guaranteed that he would not miss training.

The star was developing a reputation as something of a prima donna, but he was back just a few months later to great fanfare. "I will give my best at all times," the player promised.

He was warned by skipper Seak Poh Leong: "We are happy he is back. But he has to work hard to adjust himself to our style now. He has been away for sometime and it's not easy."

It was a testament to how good the player was. He may not always have been the easiest to handle and despite all the talk of the necessity of discipline, fans, teammates, coaches and the FAS usually did what they could to get him back in the fold. In this case, he returned following a New Year gesture by Ganesan, who had known the player since he was a young boy. "I am happy that we have managed to have this amicable meeting to clear our differences. Dollah has still a few more years of good soccer."

For the national team, it was four, as he retired in 1979 after suffering a second shoulder dislocation.

Jeffrey Low, a veteran sports writer, wrote a tribute to the former international in *The Straits Times*. It was one of the most touching and heartfelt pieces of writing that has ever appeared in print about a football player, a part of which is reproduced below:

Don't worry, my friend. We can see you in your dancing boots, jinking all the way to heaven, to the rhythm of one of your all-time favourite songs, pointing to us that, yes, on this day you should be on the bus, too.

"*And at Shah Alam for tomorrow's veterans' match against Selangor, Soh Chin Aun will be there, the one you took such great pleasure in beating. And so would Santokh Singh, who used to shout at you: 'Come lah! You dare?'*

"*Many had tried to break your legs. But all had failed. Many have tried to imitate you. None have succeeded.*

"*For there can only be one 'Gelek King', one Dollah Kassim, the one who rose from a scrawny 12-year-old juggling ragged balls in the back alleys of Farrer Park, to one of the greatest legends in the annals of local football.*

"*Proud were we to own you, a son of the soil whose greatest moments were reserved for the National Stadium's sacred turf, where the Kallang Roar erupted for you and the gang of the seventies.*

SOH CHIN AUN

The Boss. Enough said. The defender was there for pretty much all of Malaysia's best moments. He was there when Malaysia qualified for the 1972 Olympics and there when the country did it again in 1980. He was there when the Harimau Muda won bronze at the 1974 Asian

Games and there to help lift the Merdeka Cup and take gold at the SEA Games. At the time, it must have seemed like he would always be there.

There are many great things about this player, but one of the best is that nobody can agree on how many times he pulled on that famous old jersey. If you examine different sources you get figures of 324, 252, 198 and others. In the second decade of the twenty-first century, truth and facts have become a little less clear than in the past, but one thing is clear—this is a man who has played international football more than any other, even if some of those games were less "official" than some of the jerseys of European football teams that you can buy in Petaling Street Market in Kuala Lumpur.

As well as a mighty international career, he spent the seventies with Selangor, helping the Red Giants to all kinds of success. He ended his career with a stint in his home state of Melaka.

He was a defender who achieved a level of consistency that was barely believable and a longevity that is legendary. In 1971, Wales toured Australia, New Zealand and also Malaysia. It was one of those tours that were not full international games, which helps to explain why the defender never got as many caps as he could have. Wayne Jones played in attack for the Welsh that day and was full of praise for the Malaysian. "He never gave me a moment's peace and he was everywhere," said Jones who played for Bristol Rovers. "He is good enough to play in England but I am quite happy he is here and not there! He is an intelligent player and reads the game well."

There was plenty of respect for Chin Aun. *The New Nation* wrote effusively about this influential defender, calling him "the Maestro". "It is best to call him the trigger. For when it is pulled, a chain reaction is set off. The trigger hits Wong Choon Wah, the hammer. And then goes the bullet, Mokhtar Dahari. Sometimes even Choon Wah and Mokhtar look like puppets on Chin Aun's strings." This is powerful stuff, even if the newspaper went on to say that the star was, temporarily at least, losing his powers.

"He was a leader and has this presence," said Zainal Abidin Hassan. "I was lucky to have such a role model playing right in front of my eyes. You couldn't help but learn from him and the way he kept a cool head, even when the pressure was on. That is the real talent, to be able to slow things down when everything is happening around you. He was a giant of Malaysian football."

What is striking about this former defender when he talks now is his

The Stars: Fandi, SuperMokh and the Rest

clarity of thought. You can understand how youngsters such as Zainal must have felt when lining up against him. "He gave you confidence and when he was on the pitch, you felt that everything would be OK."

Soh is a man of action, the kind that Malaysian football could do with now. "It is not about saying what you are going to do," he said in 2016. "It is about showing it. You need to have dedication, you need to have determination so that you will be able to achieve what you want to. What is more important for us in this country, we have so many races ... what is more important if we can work together in order to achieve what we wanted. And that is how we qualified for the Olympics.

"We had real unity in the team, this was the most important thing. That is what we are trying to teach the young generation today, that we are united in Malaysia.

"If we don't have the players who want to play for the country, want to fight and have passion, how can we improve? Look at the Koreans and Japanese. Even today, we don't talk about qualifying for the Olympics, we talk about Southeast Asian Games. Don't talk about Thailand, no way we can beat them, look at the Vietnamese, look at Myanmar, and for that matter Indonesia. We have a big problem."

That has been the case ever since the Boss hung up his boots.

AWANG BAKAR

According to his brother, the Singapore striker wasn't always that into football. Perhaps he was one of those players who can take it or leave it. If that is true, then it is even more tragic that his dedication to Singapore football and the team played a part, at least, in his early death.

That came on 1 July 1964 when the player, probably 34 (though nobody can say for certain, as some list him as 28) collapsed during a game for Changi Malays. He was rushed to hospital, but died shortly after. In June, he had lost up to 10kg thanks to an intensive daily training routine at Farrer Park as he tried to get back into the Singapore squad.

Just two days before his death, Choo Seng Quee, familiar with the player, paid tribute to his efforts to trim a frame that had reached 75kg (165lbs). That does not seem like much in the modern game, but Awang's prime fighting weight had been around 61kg (135lbs), a weight that thanks to his Farrer Park exertions, he was 4kg short of.

"Awang starts training at Farrer Park at 2pm and keeps going at it till late in the evening," Choo enthused to *The Straits Times*. "I am giving him all the assistance and encouragement he needs because I am confident he still has a lot of good football in him."

He was due for a trial for Singapore later in July. Chief selector P. Suppiah said that it was too soon to give a trial in June. "The coaches feel that if he is tried out too soon and fails to impress the selectors, it would be a big blow to Awang Bakar. They are confident Awang Bakar will be fit and ready for a trial in three weeks."

Choo certainly was and was confident that by then, the striker would be "the Awang Bakar of old".

But who was the Awang Bakar of old, a player whose age no one was sure of? Was he born in 1930 or 1936? Early in his career, most reports had him at the earlier date, but later it changed. Given the fact that he scored six goals in three matches for RAF Changi Sailing Club in the SAFA league in 1948, then surely it was the former. That feat was impressive enough for an 18 year-old and surely beyond the means of someone not even in his teens.

At that age, he was already showing the predatory skills in the box that are hard to teach. How to be in the right place at the right time; how to anticipate where the rebound was going to fall; where the defender would try to pass; and how he was able to find time in the maelstrom of a big game to pick his spot and slot his shot home.

"I remember that while he was alive, he tried to teach shooting to us. He would demonstrate how to score ten times out of ten," his younger brother Kamisan Bakar recalled after his death. "But we were never able to understand the way he did it. I guess it was all part of his nature. It was inbuilt. He started kicking a ball around our backyard in Changi and picking up soccer tips in Kota Raja Malay School, where he studied for a few years."

His background stood him in good stead, and in February 1950 he got the call to play for Singapore, making his debut a month later as the Lions lost 2-0 to Army-Navy. Later that year, he was winning the Malaya Cup for Singapore, scoring the second goal in a 2-0 win over Penang in the final. The shot was a volley from well outside the area, following a goal kick. It silenced the majority of the 15,000 or so fans at the Malaya district ground in Rifle Range Road in Kuala Lumpur.

It was telling that *The Straits Times* described the goal—a 40-yard shot that flew back over the hapless goalkeeper's head—as a typical Bakar effort. For a player that was barely out of his teens, to have a cup final described in such terms is testament to how highly-rated he was at the time. So good and memorable was the strike that it would be referenced when talking about subsequent cup finals for years to come.

He had already forged quite a reputation for himself with his goal-scoring exploits and he tried to explain his style of play. "Courage comes first in football," he said in May 1950. "A *tidak apa* ['it doesn't matter'] attitude would be ruinous. I'm not inclined to dribble, because dribbling means wasting time and a centre-forward can't afford to do that. When he gets the ball he just shoot at goal immediately if he can, or pass it if he can't."

He was ranked second in the 1950 Malaya's Sportsman of the Year by *The Sunday Times*. First was Tho Fook Jung of Penang, the champion weightlifter of the British Empire who was nicknamed "The Toy Battleship". Reports suggested that had he participated in the world championships that year then he would have done well. Still, to come second in an award that is inherently biased in favour of individual athletes is impressive. So much so that *The Sunday Times* acknowledged that many felt that the striker should have been first.

His tendency to shine in the big games was evident once again the following year as he scored a hat-trick in a 6-0 win in the Malaya Cup final over Perak. *The Straits Times* memorably described the performance. "But for all that there were attacks that stretched the Perak defence to the limit. Awang Bakar on the hunt with all his usual gay abandon was making Lauder dive, leap and go through a series of gymnastics to keep his charge safe… Bakar was himself again, the split-second opportunist, hitting the ball with tremendous power and heading with all his old certainty and precision." They don't write match reports like that anymore.

Awang followed his hat-trick with two crucial goals in the 3-2 win over Penang at the 1952 final, marking a third Malaya Cup final in which he scored. He made the final the following year as Penang took revenge with a 3-2 win, and then his form started to suffer.

In 1955 he retired, in a move that turned out to be temporary. In 1957 he was back with the Police team, with fans and media agog as to whether this former sharpshooter—who was still only in his twenties—could make a comeback. There were signs that he could, and with Singapore lacking a centre-forward, his return was eagerly awaited. But while he did return, injuries reduced his impact.

Awang achieved so much but at times, according to his brother, his love for football was questionable. "Awang was not always keen on football. He could easily be distracted. Sometimes he was too lazy to turn up for training. At other times he was completely slack."

Perhaps if that attitude had persisted, he would have lived a lot longer. But when the mood was upon him, then he could be as single-minded in his desire to work as he was in front of goal. With that Singapore squad place within reach, he could not stop training.

"For three solid months he trained agonisingly hard," said his brother. "Each day, he woke up at 5.30am and ran for five miles (eight km). Then he went to work. At 2pm he did body-breaking physical workouts. At 5pm it was ball training, for two hard hours."

After his weight loss, all felt that Awang's comeback would be a success. "Then it came as a moment of horror when he collapsed and died—the result of heart failure brought about by over-strain." It cut his football career short but it was still a career worth writing about.

ZAINAL ABIDIN HASSAN

The man who played almost 140 games for Malaysia throughout the eighties and much of the nineties has coached three famous old Super League clubs: Selangor, Pahang and Penang.

It was at the first two where he became seriously famous as a player.

Zainal Abidin Hassan has packed plenty into his career, both as a legendary player in Malaysian football and now as a coach. He still found time to sit down with *FourFourTwo* to discuss his career on both sides of the white line. With over 130 games for his country and a playing career that spanned two decades before he took up coaching, there was plenty to talk about.

"I always knew I wanted to be a football player," he said with a twinkle in his eye. "As far as I can remember. My two brothers represented the country. They are my role models and I followed in their footsteps. It was destiny. My target was always to be a footballer."

As well as the brothers, there was also plenty of inspiration on the pitch as he started developing into a fine football player as a teenager in the mid-seventies. There were giants in action every weekend in stadiums around Malaysia.

"When I was 10 or 12, I could go to the stadium to watch international and domestic games. At the time there were huge players who were very good, but the one I always wanted to watch was the late Mokhtar Dahari."

The striker was one of the very few players who had an even bigger claim to legend status, and the seventies was a time for heroes. "The best part was when I was watching him, as well as Dato Soh Chin Aun, Santokh Singh and Arumugam and then soon after, I was shocked to be in the same team as them."

Significant steps were taken on the path towards that dream as he started to realise that he had the talent. "I chose a school, Maxwell Secondary School, which at that time [was] in Selangor and now [is] in KL," he said with a chuckle in reference to the spread of the Malaysian capital. "It was good in sport and the master of football was a good coach. When I was, I think, 15, I was representing the Selangor state schools. I was recognised and got better training and my basic skills improved."

In the late seventies, he joined Selangor as a youth player, making his debut against Sarawak in 1980. "We beat them. That was the middle of the season as I had spent a lot of time on the bench. From then, I was playing well. I don't know if I was a good player, but I worked really, really hard and then I not only met my heroes but I was playing with them and it was a shock."

Mokhtar was the one he was really looking forward to lining up with. "His playing was nothing less than 150 percent. He trained so hard and he liked to teach people, but not only him. The old players could be harsh when they spoke, but you took it and you improved and then they kept on teaching. You listened and you improved. That was the way it worked. I was lucky to have such role models in front of me."

At the time, Zainal was a full-back. "I was very fast and the duty they give you, you have to do it. I had no chance to play upfront and because of my size, I was too small to defend in the middle. I started playing full-back.

"In my era, the overlapping system was just starting. I was doing that. Modern football was coming in slowly so I kept on doing that and practicing individually and with the senior players. It was hard in Malaysia to be a modern full-back, you had to be really fit. Roberto Carlos was starting in the eighties, [also] Maldini, and these were my role models. I was lucky to have some good coaches. People like Santokh guiding me. I had so many role models in front of my eyes."

Zainal's club, position and entire career changed in 1983 when he left Selangor to play for Pahang, a route that he would become familiar with over the years. Frank Lord was the English coach. "In my first day of training, after 15 minutes, the coach stopped me and said, 'You are not a defender.' As a kid I knew that the best part of football was to score goals, so I had played in attack but only when I was young. This is what the coach told me."

"He was a typical English coach and there was not much overlapping in English football at the time. Every time we attacked, I was up there and up and down, I was young and fit enough. Lord saw me, with my skill. He made me to understand my role and turned me into a number 10. The running into space and scoring goals and being in the right position, he taught me a lot. With my speed, I could do it perfectly and after eight games I became the top goal scorer."

Zainal scored 13 goals in his first season on the east coast as he established himself as one of the best attackers in Southeast Asia. "I kept changing between Pahang and Selangor in my career. After three years at Pahang, I came back to Selangor as I wanted to play alongside Mohktar Dahari. When I came back, I made a record in the league in terms of goals."

The golden age of the national team was coming to an end, but still Malaysia was a force in the eighties. "We could beat the best teams," said Zainal. "My best memory was scoring against Saudi Arabia in 1983 as we won 3-1. That time they had Majed Abdullah, the 'Pele of the Desert', and they were a good team."

He also has regrets. "I missed the 1986 World Cup. We were just one hurdle away from getting to the final stage. We beat South Korea here and a draw in Korea would have been enough. We lost 2-0. They went to Mexico and they were a good team.

"That is the closest we came. I think five players could not make it. We recalled a goalkeeper and a few players, our best keeper Arumugan had an accident. Mokhtar was recalled after retiring. We didn't have a solid team and there were some some internal problems. There were tears in the dressing room. If we had a full team then we could have done it.

"I served the country for almost 20 years. I was 37. In the seventies and eighties it was about how skilful you are, but now it is about how fast you are. Then you could hold the ball and look around but now there is no chance. Players need to be quick.

"The game in Malaysia has got faster. If I had my speed, I would enjoy playing now. There was not much protection from referees back then."

CHAPTER 7

FOREIGN
INFLUENCE:
SINGAPOREAN STYLE

You cannot compare Singapore with Malaysia, as we do not have
a huge base to choose from. We also do not have many teams in
our league. What is wrong selecting naturalised players to play for
Singapore? If they can improve our football, then why not?

—Radojko "Raddy" Avramović,
former Singapore coach

Given their strategic locations at the heart of Southeast Asia, in the
middle of one of the busiest shipping lanes in the world, a bridge
between China and India and between East Asia and Europe and the
Middle East, it is no surprise that Malaysia and Singapore have long
been cosmopolitan places.

Singapore especially has become an international hub in business,
finance and trade. A relatively high proportion of the city state is home
to people from all over the world in a bid to help what is, after all, a
little red dot compete with the rest of Asia and the world.

It was no surprise, then, that something similar happened in the
world of sport. Governments, media and people all over the world love
success in that field. At one time, countries like the United Kingdom
used to mock communist competitors for focusing resources in order
to win gold medals at the Olympics. These successes were seen as
validation of the political system and useful propaganda tools. However,
after gaining gold just once at the 1996 Atlanta Olympics, Great Britain
resolved never to be so humiliated on the sporting stage again, and
funds and programmes were set up. By 2016, the country was second in
the medal table and the former mocking of the likes of the Soviet Union
and East Germany seems a little ironic now—but it shows that sport is

important, especially when you are doing badly.

In Singapore, the Foreign Sports Talent Scheme was introduced in 1993 by the country's table tennis association, who felt that importing players would raise standards all round. The trail blazed by ping-pong was soon followed by football, the most popular and international team sport in the world.

It stood to reason that the FAS wanted to get a piece of the action. By 2002, the first foreign-born Lions were drafted into the national team. There was Mirko Grabovac from Croatia, England's Daniel Bennett and Egmar Gonçalves, born in Brazil.

Naturalising players who were born overseas is a big move and it can change the character of the whole national team. Some countries do it a little, some a lot and some don't do it at all.

As we saw earlier, there has been some controversy over the use of foreign-born players in the Singapore team. Malaysia captain Safiq Rahim was especially vocal after the first leg of their World Cup qualifier back in 2011, but the star may have just been voicing his frustration after losing 5-3.

"I know that people said these things in Malaysia," said Durić. "I knew some people were against it, but the world is changing. You see in England and Scotland, where the mothers and fathers are born in different countries but they live there and call it home and then play for the national team. You can't stop those kids and we have to follow or we will be left behind."

Singapore has a population that is around a fifth of the size of its neighbour. It is easy to understand that there has been a desire to widen the player pool.

As a country that is exceptionally international by nature, perhaps it is only fitting that Singapore's national team reflects that character. The team is as international and as cosmopolitan as the place it represents. More of a talking point could be the fact that this a country that naturalises foreigners to play internationally because of the lack of a "huge base to choose from", but then the biggest section of that base, the ethnic Chinese community, produces nothing like the number of players that it used to.

That is a different debate. As an outsider, it is interesting that some of the players I think of first when I think of the Singapore national team were not only not born in the country, but had zero connections with it until they arrived to play football.

ALEKSANDAR DURIĆ

There are few players over the years who have worn the Singapore jersey with such pride as Aleksandar Durić, few who seemed to have the spirit of the Lion as much as the lion-hearted striker.

Durić had seen other players fast-tracked via the FAS's Foreign Talent Scheme, which whizzed them through the citizenship application process so they could go and play for the national team.

Born in Bosnia (then a part of Yugoslavia) in 1970, Durić is the poster child for naturalised players, not only in Southeast Asia, but around the world. Few have gone so far from their original homeland, and few have gone so far with their adopted country.

"It was back in 1999 and I was with West Adelaide in Australia's National Football League," he said. "It happened that the club was experiencing financial problems and they wanted to offload the more expensive players and I was one of them. I got a call from my agent friend and they said there was a club in Singapore that needed strikers."

It could have been different. He could have become a legend of football in Hong Kong. But he chose the former British colony further to the south rather than the Special Administrative Region. One of the reasons he headed there was because this "little Hong Kong club" asked for a trial. "I wasn't happy about that as I was an experienced professional."

He was not an experienced striker, however, and that is what Tanjong Pagar wanted. "I was mostly an attacking midfielder or on the left side of midfield but my agent told me not to worry about that. He told me that I would pass as a striker, no problem."

That wasn't the only issue. "I didn't even know that Singapore had a professional league. That was on my mind as I was flying towards Singapore, I just didn't know what to expect."

Sometimes that can be the best way. "To be honest, I was surprised at the standard as the S-League was really good. We all know that it has gone down in recent years. But this was in the first years of the league and there was a kind of rush about the place. The fans were coming to the games, there was more money around then than today, there was a very good mixture of foreign and local players. The foreign players then were really good and many had played at a high level and they came in their thirties.

"It took me sometime to understand the kind of football that was being played. You could see the difference in the teams coached by foreigners and the playing style with those coached by locals. The local coaches were mostly focused on playing a more physical game and the foreign coaches were more interested in a technical game. There was an interesting mixture of teams and styles. Technically, the local players of that generation were pretty good, like Fandi. There was much more freedom at that time to express yourself than there is now. I really enjoyed it."

Durić has seen both sides of the coin: years in the S-League as a foreigner and then years in the S-League as a Singaporean. The pressures on imports are immense.

As a journalist who has been writing about football in Asia since the last millennium, some things have not changed and the challenges to foreign players who come to various Asian leagues is one of those constants. Back in England and back in the old days before the English Premier League became the richest in the world, foreign players were rare beasts. If we take the Scots, Welsh and Irish out of the equation then all that was left was an occasional Scandinavian. I remember when Bryan Roy signed for Nottingham Forest in the summer of 1994. The winger was not the greatest player to come from the Netherlands but there was excitement that a Dutch international, one that had just impressed at the World Cup, was joining a team that had just been promoted.

So foreigners were, for a time, real curiosities, especially when they came from countries than had a reputation for flair. Then they became ubiquitous to the extent that they first lost their novelty value and then started to outnumber the locals. Also, England had not just gone for the top-end of talent from overseas; those a little lower down the scale are seen as cheaper alternatives to overpriced local players.

Not so in Singapore and Malaysia. They are also—on the whole— considerably more expensive than the homegrown stars, but that brings expectations.

Almost no import has any idea of what to expect in terms of culture and lifestyle when they come to Southeast Asia, and that can be an exciting thing. The ones that embrace their new homes off the pitch, or at least arrive with an open mind, are those that tend to do better on the pitch and stay for longer.

But it is not easy. "As foreign players, we were expected to do everything, sometimes they even expect you to be a goalkeeper!" Durić laughs. "I had the feeling from the start that expectations were so high, but then the salaries were not always so high. In 1999, when I came, they were famous for changing players after two weeks with no rules or regulations. Even if you sign a contract for 12 months then you can be out after two games because of people who don't like you, even though they don't like or know football.

"I got used to it over the years, to be constantly [under] pressure from the day I arrived until the day I retired. As a sportsman, you always have to be under pressure to perform well but that kind of pressure, not many players can survive. Lots of imports come and go. They tell me they have no idea how I survived all of those years."

I have known foreigners referred to as "bonus bank" by teammates who saw them as players to score goals and win games and earn them bonus win payments. And there have been those from abroad who make little attempt to learn the names of their teammates and spend little time getting to know them or mix with them. Unless you are a special player, you have to make the effort with your teammates.

Durić continued: "I was lucky, I had played in a few countries and I had a basic motto that applied on and off the pitch. I tried to adapt to that country and the culture as much as possible and you have to respect the people and to become part of the place and contribute. There is no point in saying that you are a star and that you don't mix with your teammates. I saw that happen sometimes and sometimes it works, but most of the time you are asking for trouble. To bring the players and fans on your side, you have to play well and you can't hide, you have to show that talent as well as the fact you are hard-working and show your skills at dribbling and free-kicks.

"During my first game, I heard comments that said, 'go back to where you came from, you ugly foreigner'. It wasn't nice to hear that, but it is a game and there is a lot of emotion. Southeast Asia is a very hard place for foreign players to play. Singapore players don't go out to play in another country, so they don't know what it is like for foreign players. I always told them that if you go overseas to play, you will understand how foreign players feel. There are cultural issues that you have to deal with."

But the best foreign players want to make a difference in terms of scoring goals and winning games by helping the locals change, develop and improve. This can be Eric Cantona or Arsene Wenger in the English Premier League, or it can be Aleksandar Durić in Singapore.

Wenger had huge influence in England, especially in the fields of diet, nutrition, sports science and all the rest. Cantona had an effect, not least, by showing a generation of young English footballers that players have to take responsibility to become as good as they possibly can be. Durić did his best.

"When I arrived, in the first months I knew that if I followed the coaching methods that were being used at Tanjong Pagar, my career would have been over pretty soon. The style of the training and commitment, I always felt was so low. The intensity of the training was so low. If I didn't work extra by myself then I would have had problems. There is always a danger for foreign players that they follow the training set by the clubs and their level drops and they don't even realise. Before you know it, you have dropped down to such a level that you are sacked as you are being paid more than the local players. That was an issue then and nothing has changed now.

"The local players feel that it is a hobby, not something to feed the kids and take care of their mum and dad. They can't feel this is their profession. It is a risky business and you have to be 100 percent ready for every session and every game.

"I was the only one to do the extra training. They used to call me crazy but after a while some of them told me that they now know what I was talking about. I lasted until I was 44 and I was stronger than all of them and I wanted to show them. A few followed a little, but not really. I was practicing shooting, crossing, running and all the rest. They did not pick it up. There is so much going on in Singapore."

Durić has naturalised as smoothly as seems possible, though it obviously takes hard work and a certain attitude. Others did not find it so easy.

MIRKO GRABOVAC AND EGMAR GONÇALVES

Naturalisation is a seductive idea for both player and federation, especially when there is the prospect of having a player in the national team who looks like he is going to score shedloads of goals. Perhaps, then, the rather abstract notion of what naturalising means for the sporting identity of a nation does not seem quite so important. Even those who are against such an idea would still likely be cheering on the new man if he was to score the winning goal in an AFF Suzuki Cup final.

When success is within reach then even countries that had previously prided themselves on never even contemplating such a policy can start to think the unthinkable. During an uncertain qualification for the 2014 World Cup, the Korean Football Association (KFA) tried to fast-track Eninho into the national team. The Brazilian was playing for one of Asia's leading clubs, Jeonbuk Motors, and with a place in Brazil in the balance, it was felt that he could help the team's chances. While the support among fans was mixed, the KFA was determined to push on, and it was only when the application was refused by the government that it all ended.

Mirko Grabovac had scored plenty of goals in the S-League. He was named the competition's player of the decade—not season—in 2005 after his exploits with SAFFC and Tampines Rovers. The 244 goals he has scored in the league remain to this day the second highest total, and he was the league's top scorer on no less than five occasions. In the end, he won four S-League titles, three Singapore Cups and one ASEAN Club Championship. It remains an impressive record.

When the idea of playing for Singapore was mooted to Grabovac and Egmar Gonçalves early in the new millennium, both were open—after all, neither was going to be playing for his home nation. Singapore offered a chance of international football and a possible route to the World Cup, however tenuous that route might be. In 2000, the Lions had lost the Tiger Cup they had last won in 1998. With these new recruits, then surely there would be more silverware? But if you are giving people passports to play football, what are they going to do when their football career finishes? These are people that have families and ties elsewhere in the world. The idea that people may stay for as long as they can play but then go home as soon as they hang up their international boots, was something that was a concern.

John Koh, then the FAS Chief Operating Officer, told *The New Paper* in 2002 that there would be a role for the players when they finished their international careers. "No, they are not here just to play for Singapore and then pack up when it's all over," he said. "We have a scheme to help them in their career choices when their playing days are over. It will depend on their choices and aptitude."

He added they could become administrative officials, but that could mean missing out on their real talents. "The most logical choice is coaching. There is a dearth of quality coaches, especially in schools and youth programs. With their backgrounds and experience as top players here in the S-League, they would be a hit with children taking up the game. They could even become specialist coaches, since they are both strikers."

It did not turn out the way that the player, his wife and the FAS hoped. This striker, who had scored a crazy amount of goals in the S-League and looked to be far and away the biggest goal threat on the island, flopped for the national team. In 12 appearances, Grabovac failed to score a single goal.

In 2008, at the age of 37, Grabovac's time as an S-League player came to an end and instead of staying and coaching, he gave up his red passport and headed back home to Croatia. It was an understandable move, though helping out at his wife's bakery was probably not what was on his mind.

He had been living in Singapore for some time while his family remained in Europe, so it was always likely that he was not going to stay.

"I don't know if I'm happy, sad, disappointed. I will miss many friends here in Singapore," he said at the time. "If I married a Singaporean here, it would have been easier to stay on. But I came to Singapore already married."

He added: "In 2001, after coming here in 1999, my wife and I really could see our future in Singapore. She speaks perfect English and can easily get a job here. Who doesn't want to live in Singapore? It's a nice place, we made many friends here, the education system is good, and it's very safe. From the money I earned here, I have a house and an apartment back in Croatia, so my life will be okay."

The problem is that local players often struggle financially when their careers end in Singapore. It is no secret that salaries are not especially high, but living costs certainly are. Grabovac faced similar problems.

"I only wish I had more options to consider before leaving Singapore, because even here, the career and financial path in football after you finish playing is limited because of the budgets. I'm like any normal family man, I have to make a safety net for my family. I'm open to negotiations after a few years, but after my playing days were over, I felt there was nothing much for me to consider. I originally came here for football, so who knows, one day, I may come back with my family again to work in Singapore, when my daughters are much older."

He did not, or at least has not, yet. Life has a habit of getting in the way.

It shows the convenient nature of naturalisation. You would hope that all who take the passport have a special feeling for Singapore. If you live somewhere long enough (now FIFA says it must be a residential period of five years) then it would be strange if you did not have some kind of bond with your new home. Whether that translates into something approaching patriotism is a different debate. For some, it seems to do just that; for others, it is fun while it lasts but they quickly move on when it ends.

That is what happened with Gonçalves. The Brazilian's situation was not so different to his Croatian counterpart. He scored an amazing 238 goals in the league during 11 seasons with Home United. Such firepower would surely give the Lions a much more potent bite. He was called up at the same time as Grabovac in 2002 and scored four goals in 15 games, a much better return than his new compatriot—but still not one to write home about, whether to Rio or anywhere else.

In 2007 he left, was branded a mercenary and a traitor, and sneaked out of the airport to return home. "Tell me, how do I stay here with no job?" he asked reporter Chia Siang Yee. "I have one big family. How do I stay here with no job? That's my question to people who say that [I am a traitor]. When my contract ended, nobody said anything to me, even though I wanted to stay, [and] I could still play."

He had become surplus to requirements at his club. "Things happened, I had no choice. My contract ended and there was no intent from the club to extend it. I even stayed two months after my contract ended but no, no one from the club spoke to me about a new contract.

"Only the coach, Vincent Subramaniam, approached me and told me maybe the club had to lower my salary. I told him it would be difficult. I have three children to feed. It's not easy. How would you feel after giving your best for 11 years? After the coach came, the club didn't say anything else. Until now, I still feel angry and hard done by. That's why I packed up and go [sic]."

There were some regrets.

"Maybe we could've discussed how much they wanted to cut my salary and explain to me the circumstances. Maybe then we could have worked something out. If I had known the reason behind the pay cut, I'd sign on as long as it wasn't too much. But they (club chairman and manager) didn't come.

"I don't care if people say I am money-minded. I just care about playing football. Everyone has his price. I gave my best to Home. I only found it unfair that they wanted to touch my salary. But what's done is done. My mother had been yearning for me to go back to Brazil. She wanted to see her grandchildren and I thought perhaps it was best for me to return."

Gonçalves return home spelled the start of a debate about the benefits of naturalising players.

The departures had fans asking whether Durić would do the same, but there was a difference as the big striker had not been part of the fast-track scheme like the other two goal-getters. There was no such contact coming his way and he decided to start the process himself. It was not an easy one. He was rejected twice, but it was a case of third time lucky.

"I am not going to give up my passport because I am totally different from Egmar and Mirko," he said. "My case was different and I came through on my own. It didn't really work for Grabovac and Gonçalves and they left. It was probably because they had always been told that they deserved to play all the time and they didn't like being on the bench or being changed by Raddy. Raddy was old school and liked discipline. He expected players to listen and obey and if they could not fit into his play then he would find someone who could. I played with him from day one and we retired together. I knew what he was all about—his philosophy was that you may be a striker, but you are there for the team. They couldn't seem to fit into that. I am not sure what went wrong but that was a factor."

Durić was different. Three years shy of 40 by the time he became a Singapore citizen, he was at an age when most footballers were thinking of retiring instead of starting out on an international career.

"I wanted to become a Singapore citizen. I had travelled around the world and never settled in any place more than one or two seasons. When I arrived in 1999 to 2006, when I started applying, I really felt that Singapore was coming into my heart. I started making friends here. My kids were born here, all three. I spent the best time of my life in Singapore and I was still there. I just thought, I have an Aussie passport and everyone told me that I was crazy. They said, 'You have an Aussie passport, plus you are not educated enough. You are not a doctor or something else in high demand.' I applied a few times and I was rejected, but I never gave up. I eventually became a citizen and I am a proud Singaporean. I have been working for the Ministry of Sport and they tell me that I am a good Singaporean."

Just a few weeks after his successful application, the call-up came. He joined his first squad to take on Tajikistan for qualification for the 2010 World Cup. The coach at the time was Radojko Avramović who hailed from the same part of Europe as his new striker. Durić does not believe that the Balkan connection played a part in the coach's decision and while it can't have hurt, few who had seen him in the S-League over the years or would see him playing for the national team would disagree.

"I selected him because his performances deserved a place in the Singapore team," Avramović said by phone from Europe. "It was that simple. I felt he would improve the team. I felt that he would score goals and also be a leader on the pitch." His age was not an issue. "Of course, we knew that this was not going to be a long-term solution in attack. Durić was not going to be playing five years later but in the short-term, he had a big part to play on many levels."

Raddy could not have been more right. Durić took to life in the national team with the same zest, energy and determination he had shown throughout his time in Singapore. The call-up is something that the striker will never forget.

"I came into training one day. It was in the best year I had in my football career, 2007. It was an incredible year. We won the league with games to spare and we won the cup and everything. I scored 44 goals and I was flying and we were flying. I had really good players around me. I was the captain but we had many captains.

"In September I became a citizen. In October, I came into training and the general manager called me to the office. I thought that he wanted to talk about the team or the following season. Instead, he shook my hand and said 'congratulations'. He gave me a letter and I saw it was from FAS and the letter was calling me for a camp for a World Cup qualifier against Tajikistan. It told me when and where to go."

It sounds strange now given the success that was to come, but Durić hesitated over whether he should accept the summons. "I was shocked and my first question was whether I should really go. The GM said that it was up to me but if it was him, he would go. He said that the league is the league but you will never regret playing for the national team. I was worried as I was old at 37. I thought that the international team was calling me as an old man."

Earning acceptance when you are not far from 40 is not easy given some of the mixed success of the naturalised players in the past. Not nervous before the game as he did not expect to start, Durić did get the call from the boss and scored both goals in a 2-0 win at the National Stadium. He played for five more years without missing a single game and became Singapore's first ever foreign-born captain.

What was perhaps most impressive is that he became so well-loved in his new home—but such was his determination to serve Singapore well on and off the pitch, that made as much of a difference as his goal-scoring talents.

"I couldn't wait for my chance to prove to the fans how much I cared about Singapore by playing my heart out on the field. I would show them how much it meant to me to represent the country." In terms of attitude and professionalism, Durić really was the example and influence that Raddy had hoped for.

"But the players were all guys I played with and against in the league. There was a welcoming feeling in the camp and that was lucky. It helped me to get settled and in just one session, I was part of them.

"The first time I heard the national anthem it was a big shock. It took me a while to learn the words and understand it all, as they sing it in Malay. It was a mixture of emotion, looking at the flag and then listening to the other players around me singing. At the same time I was so proud to be standing with great players and I thought I will play a few games and never be called again. I was determined to use every opportunity to give my best.

"What a debut it was. I could have played for three days, not 90 minutes. We qualified for the next round for the first time and it was a big thing.

"I played 54 times in the end and scored 27 goals and retired on a high note. I scored at the AFF Suzuki Cup in 2012 and we won the tournament. We won, not because of me, but because we had a great team, great support and a great dressing room. Nobody gave us a chance and it was great to prove people wrong."

JOHN WILKINSON

John Wilkinson met his wife in Singapore on the first day he arrived back in 2003. He had been playing for Exeter in the lower leagues of England but injuries intervened and threatened to end a career that was just getting started.

"I tore my knee ligaments while playing for Exeter City, then broke my ankle nine months later during my first full training session back," he said. There were spells with Shrewsbury and then Bohemians in Ireland. Actually, before the call came to go to Southeast Asia, he had been thinking of giving up the game completely.

"An agent contacted a couple of the former Man United players newly signed by Exeter City, Graham Tomlinson and Neil Whitworth, about the possibility of them playing in Singapore; they declined but mentioned my name as someone who might be interested. Venga, the General Manager of Woodlands Wellington, met me in Leeds and I signed."

They thought the midfielder was a striker and he was not about to let a small detail like that get in the way of an exciting opportunity. And he never looked back. The year was 2002.

It was a journey from West Yorkshire to Southeast Asia, and then plenty more besides. "It felt a long way away from what I was used to, on and off the pitch."

Yet football is football and once the action kicked off, it all came flooding back. It helped that the S-League was a more vibrant place back then. "The fans were terrific in those days, I always had a good relationship with fans of the clubs I played for. Stadiums used to be full and noisy."

Professional, hard-working and dedicated, the Englishman soon became a favourite at Woodlands Wellington. Then came the possibility of adding international football to what was becoming an interesting resume.

"I got a phone call from Venga [R. Vengadasalam, a colourful former manager of Woodlands] in my first season explaining about the Foreign Talent Scheme and asking if I was interested. I was 22 years old and had no plans to settle in Singapore ... or anywhere really."

The issue was not taken further but was raised again by then national team coach Raddy in 2005. This time Wilkinson was more interested. "I started making arrangements to try and get citizenship before the AFF Suzuki Cup 2007 but missed [it] by weeks." Watching Singapore go on to lift the trophy only served as inspiration for the player.

Changing nationality when far from home is a complex thing to do. Not only are there the concerns of local fans to worry about and how they will take to a foreigner becoming a Singaporean international, the reactions of family back home can be important, too. This wasn't an issue in Wilkinson's case.

"They weren't really bothered, to be honest with you, I don't think it really registered with them. I was a long way away and since the passing of my father when I was a teenager none of my family took an interest in my professional career."

With no concerns about how family back home was taking his

decision, the focus was on getting to grips with his new football family. But he was accepted smoothly by his new international teammates.

"I was coming into the national setup on the back of winning the S-League title with SAF and we were comfortably the best club side in the region at that point," recalls Wilkinson. "The boys knew that I wasn't put on the Foreign Talent Scheme and given some money to jump in with them—I know that some of the local-born players resented the fact that some players were given a financial package to take up citizenship. I thought long and hard about it and arranged everything myself. I felt welcome."

The big question—at least for me—is how Singaporean does a naturalised player actually feel? Is it possible to feel patriotism for a new country? Wilkinson's answer gives an interesting perspective on the whole issue. Basically, it takes time.

"I didn't feel any great emotion upon hearing the national anthem in the beginning because I just simply hadn't fought any on-field battles yet. The more games we won, the longer we were holed up away from our families, the more the sense of patriotism upon hearing the anthem would kick in ... Running fights in the tunnel with the likes of Jordan would only serve to heighten the emotion I felt when hearing the anthem ... it always got me at it, sometimes it would get me too hyped and I'd have to try and calm myself down."

This was not a player who took appearing for his new national team lightly. Perhaps it is the case that, often, the new boys are keener to succeed than the natives. Wilkinson succeeded while bigger S-League stars such as Grabovac and Gonçalves failed, although the problem with being a striker is that a quick glance at the goals scored column quickly gives a good indication of how things are going.

"I was a wide or central midfielder whose game was all about energy and appetite—that fitted well into the team at the time. I'm also married to a Singaporean who had worked within the football fraternity, so that helped. Mirko and Egmar were in a poorer national team than the one I stepped into and they were strikers that needed service—I don't think they got much of that."

DANIEL BENNETT

Daniel Bennett has been playing for Singapore longer than most. Born in Great Yarmouth in eastern England in 1978—not one of the hotbeds of English football—he took up Singapore citizenship in 2002.

It made sense for someone who had spent part of his childhood in the country. Bennett's background was an interesting one. At the age of 15, he was a trainee with National Football League side Tiong Bahru before he headed back to England. Back in Southeast Asia in 1999, he signed for Balestier Central and then Tanjong Pagar. Then it was back to Wrexham and then relegation, a brief return to Singapore and the Singapore Armed Forces team, and then another brief return to Wrexham. That went well and he was offered a new contract to play in north Wales.

Bennett turned it down to return to the Lion City and embark on an international career that would turn out to be something special. It was Jan Poulsen who gave the big man the nod in a friendly against the Philippines in December 2002.

"I knew that he would be a good player for Singapore," said Poulsen. "There are some players who you are never sure about until they are actually on the pitch, whether in training or when the game starts. But with Bennett there was never any doubt. He may not have been the most skilful but he had everything that a coach wants in a centre-back. He had good central defensive play. He can defend but there was more than that. He had leadership, he had organisational skills and he helped others, too. He was exactly the kind of player that Singapore needed. He brought real character to the team and you always knew that he would never let you down."

And in response to some of the criticism that there were too many players naturalised in Singapore, or whether the national team should be naturalising players at all, Poulsen argues that they should judge the players by their performances.

"The number of years he has been around and the number of games he has played shows that Bennett has given everything to the national team every single time he has taken the pitch. He has sweated and given blood and taken injuries for the team. You can see this from all the coaches that have selected him and then by the fact that even at the age of 38 he was called again for the 2016 AFF Cup. He is a safe option as he does not make many mistakes. He still has the same qualities now. Nobody has had more passion to represent Singapore than Bennett."

The man himself said on radio in 2013, as he retired from the international game (though he was to return), that he often wondered what would have happened had he accepted that new offer from

Wrexham back at the start of the century. "It's always something that comes to my mind," he said. "But the draw of coming here and playing for the national team and travelling around Asia playing some of the top teams was too great to turn down. I was living in Wrexham in a small house without a car, a long way from anywhere. Playing in a fantastic stadium with fantastic support, but just to come back here where I have always lived, this is really my home and I will always live here, [and] I wouldn't change it."

So, just like calling up local-born players, you never know who will be successful—though the same can be said when a national team coach calls up any player. You never quite know who will succeed and who will not.

Bennett has a long association with Singapore. He may have been born in England but he is at least as much a Singaporean. "I had a lot of pride to play for Singapore," he said when we talked. "I grew up here. I was desperate to play for the national team. I saw myself as in between Singapore and England. When I went to England in the summer and also university, I was always from Singapore, in the eyes of others. When I was in Singapore, I was seen as an expat. That is just the way it is. This is modern society. I have a Singapore passport and my home and family is here, but there still some English in me."

He has spent his life travelling between the two countries. "I came over to Singapore when I was two years old with my parents as my dad got a job teaching here. I don't have any memories of England at the time but I can remember a bit about Singapore. We lived in houses then, as there were not many condos. We used to go back every summer holiday.

"When I graduated from school here, I went to Loughborough University." That is a famous sporting university in England and one that many athletes have passed through. "I had played in the semi-pro league in Singapore before I left and then played for the Uni. Once I finished, I had the call from a manager in Singapore and he was talking about the S-League, which was professional. I thought I could play for six months and then go and get a proper job!

"That never happened. Shortly after, they started talking about a passport. I came back in 1999, midway through the year. In 2001, I think, I had the opportunity to play against Liverpool when they came out here. I started thinking about going back to play over in England again. I sent some feelers out and was offered trials with quite a few clubs. One was Swindon Town but at the time, they couldn't sign players and this was my first club and I went to a few others. Malcolm Crosby recommended me to Wrexham and they signed me."

People who grow up in two different and distinct cultures often talk of not being completely accepted in either, as they fall between two identities. Perhaps the same is true of football, with players carrying something of each country inside them.

"I don't know if I had more of a Singapore style of play, but when I went for a few trials in England, a lot of the managers suggested that I should go to Europe as the ball was played more on the floor there. In Singapore, we didn't play as many high balls and were more focused on the technical. In the lower leagues in England it was very physical, but I enjoyed that. I think I adapted quickly.

"But the chance to play for a national team and travel around Asia and Southeast Asia and play in the AFF Suzuki Cups was an amazing one and one that anyone would have to think about. I came back and had the chance to play for different clubs and I met my wife shortly after and then had my family here."

There were other attractions too. "At that point the league was considered a very strong league in the region. And a lot of players were coming here, and they were good players—and we used to get the best Thai players."

Bennett has played more games for Singapore than any other. Not only is his passion and commitment not in any doubt, but he has seen plenty of changes. "I think the quality of foreigners coming here is nowhere near what it was. I think the leagues around, like, Malaysia and Thailand, have improved, while we have stood still. I don't think it is run as well as it was, nowhere near. We don't have the youth players coming through and we have few who can play in the national team. Khairul Amri is 32 years old and is still the best we have."

I ask if this was apparent in the fact that he was still playing for the team at the ripe old age of 38. "They shouldn't need to call me, you are right. Because of the lack of youth coming through and so I am still getting a chance, which I still enjoy. We need to get more kids, better facilities and coaching. The kids are on their iPads. The way society has changed, everyone is studying all the time. Playing fields are hard to find these days and even S-League teams are struggling. The coaching is not what it was even though more and more people get coaching licenses, but the quality is not as good as before. We need to get more ex-players in.

"We had some good games in qualifiers. We were close to qualifying for the Asian Cup." That was the 2011 version. "That is one of the biggest regrets when I look back. We had a group with Thailand, Jordan and Iran."

It was so close that a draw in the final game in Jordan would have been enough to take Singapore into the tournament. In a hostile environment on and off the pitch in Amman the Lions had equalised, but couldn't hang on and lost 2-1.

"We were very close and conceded a goal late in Jordan. It was more difficult then as there were only 16 teams. We really should have got there and that would have been a fantastic achievement."

It was already pretty impressive. Some of Asia's best teams, such as Australia and Japan, have lost World Cup qualifiers in Amman in recent years, and it remains one of the hardest places to go on the continent if you need a result. The atmosphere can be intense, the playing surface can be too, and then there are always the lasers that fans shine into the eyes of opponents. It is a test in every sense of the word and Singapore deserve credit for coming so close. If the Lions had actually made it to the Asian Cup, perhaps things wound be different now. Perhaps it would have taken Singaporean football to the next level and moved the country ahead of their rivals.

Bennett is not so sure whether it would have made a long-term difference. Failure to do so didn't necessarily mean that Singapore stalled or moved backwards. "I don't see Malaysia moving ahead of us. We have always been similar in some ways. Thailand, yes, you can see the players they have.

"They shouldn't need to call me—though you need to have experience, you need some players to guide the youngsters. When Stange was there, that was shown, as he didn't want to select older players. We struggled with that. It was shown at the 2014 Suzuki Cup. We needed to keep a clean sheet in the second half and he didn't have the players to come on, and a couple of experienced players could have made a real difference."

Maybe someone like Durić?

"Durić has to be there as the most difficult striker that I have played against in the S-League. He was so physical that you couldn't get near him. You had to keep him at arm's length so he couldn't grab you and turn you. Egmar was outstanding in the league and Therdsak was one of the best players I played with. Lee Trundle at Wrexham was another.

They were two of the most talented players I have seen. But Durić was tough. He was so alert in the box and everything came to him, all the second balls. He was a winner and that has driven him on. He is the kind of player that every team needs."

If Bennett plays until 44, as Durić did, then he could become the most capped player in international history. That really would be something.

"I looked at the top of the table at how many caps the top players have got. The top is about 180 and to be on that list with those players is an incredible feeling. I started at 25 and was left out by Stange for three years, and so it could have been a lot more, but many players can say the same. But I don't know when I will stop. My wife is sometimes on at me to give it up. I sometimes wish my legs would give up and then I could just stop. But I feel good and I am enjoying still playing and I will take it season by season."

PLAYING MALAYSIA

Durić hails from a region where local rivalries such as Serbia and Croatia run long and fierce. Malaysia and Singapore, however, also has plenty of history.

Some of his best memories came against Malaysia. "When I arrived in 1999, I always heard about Singapore and Malaysia. They told me that at club level, there was a lot of history. In the sixties, seventies and eighties, the old generation was something special and the games they played were special, too. It is great in football, this is emotion.

"Anytime you mentioned Malaysia, everyone said that we had to win. I felt that as we played against them and I have good memories. In Malaysia, they always remember me as the guy who always scored against them. These were games that I looked forward to. These are the games that every Singaporean looks forward to.

"As a rivalry, Europe is more violent than Malaysia and Singapore. It is more sporting here, as the countries want to show who is better at football. Unfortunately in Europe, it can go too far. Here, though, there is pressure on the coach. If you lose, especially by a big score, then the coach can get sacked. I was there watching in 2002 at the National Stadium when we lost 4-0 to Malaysia. It was really bad, with the fans showing that they were not happy. Jan Poulsen was fired soon after. It was all connected to this special feeling."

During John Wilkinson's time with the national team from 2007 to 2010, Singapore and Malaysia's paths did not cross often competitively. At the time, the Lions were focused on qualifying for the World Cup and were spending time preparing and training in West Asia. That meant that Wilkinson's experience of the rivalry was confined to friendlies.

"I didn't really feel the rivalry in our dressing room, it always seemed that they hated us more than the other way round."

There were a few taunts and comments from Malaysian fans about Singapore's international squad.

"Getting off the team bus I would sometimes hear things, but I was sympathetic to it. The fans still to this day live off the cross-Causeway rivalry, and it had been taken away from them for that period as they found it difficult to compete with us."

CHAPTER 8

FOREIGN INFLUENCE: THE MALAYSIA METHOD

My opinion is that you should have some type of connection with the country. I see a lot of players who go to Hong Kong and Singapore and play there for five years and then go and get naturalised and then they are happy about having an Asian passport. There should be some kind of link.

—Matthew Davies, Malaysia international right-back

Malaysia is less comfortable naturalising foreign players than Singapore. The country does, however, have a number of players who are born overseas with Malaysian heritage who represent the nation.

Like Matthew Davies. The right-back was born in Perth, on the western edge of Australia, in 1995, a relatively close five-hour flight to Kuala Lumpur—as opposed to the eight or more from cities such as Sydney or Melbourne.

"I was quite conscious of my Malaysian heritage," he said from national team duty in Manila. "The whole side of my mother's family was Malaysian. My mum was one of nine brothers and sisters and all my family would meet at Christmas and holidays. It was a big family and so Malaysia was always a part of my childhood."

Not the football team though, which is perhaps not surprising as Australia was beginning to qualify for World Cups by the time Davies started to think about a career in football. "To be honest, I did not follow the Malaysia national team. I was very focused on my own career. I was in the Australian youth set up and firmly in the Australian system."

It was going quite well when he joined the youth team of local A-League club Perth Glory. You can still, at the time of writing at least, read his reaction on the club's official website when he was first selected at the tender age of 18. "I'm ecstatic," he said, as he joined the full squad after working with Alistair Edwards, the youth coach who moved to help out at Johor Darul Ta'zim FC in the Malaysia Super League.

"It's something I've been working towards for a long time and to finally sign the paper is a good feeling. It's great to have the opportunity to work with all these experienced players and…we are trying to learn as much from them as we can and improve as much as we can."

He made his senior debut in October 2013 against Melbourne City (then known as Heart in the days before it became a part of the City Football Group, which has Manchester City as the biggest and most prominent member) in the A-League. It ended in a 1-0 win and the reviews identified Davies as a promising player.

He was also, in the same year, selected for the Under-19 Young Socceroos squad to play at a Spanish tournament in 2013—he earned three caps under coach Paul Okon—but in the end, it wasn't enough. His original chance to play in Perth's first team had come due to an injury to Josh Risdon, and while 16 senior appearances in two seasons sounds pretty good for a teenager, it just wasn't enough for a player who was in a hurry.

"I was about to head off to another A-League team," he said. "I had played two seasons for Perth and managed a few games here and there, but there just weren't many options presenting themselves and I had an established right-back ahead of me. I didn't want to wait, I was ready to get going. I wanted to play football as much as possible and did not want to stay in Australia and get only ten games of senior football a year."

Just 18 months after making his senior debut for Perth, he was playing for Pahang in the Malaysia Super League. By the time he was 21, he was captain of the *Tok Gajah* (The Elephants) and is the youngest skipper the famed east coast club has ever had.

Once the move to Malaysia was on the table, it did not take long for the player to head north.

"I realised there was a Malaysian option to follow. That was when I was around 20. It was something I was very interested in doing. My agent at the time in Australia just happened to ask me by chance, 'What is your background, by the way?' And once I told him about Malaysia, he said 'I have the perfect person for you.'"

This was Scott Ollerenshaw, a former Australian international who had played in Malaysia in the nineties, scoring plenty of goals for Sabah.

Once the ex-Socceroo hung up his boots, he stayed on the Malaysian scene to become an agent, and a well-respected one at that.

"Scott got in touch and then we took it from there. I wanted to play senior football and get 30–40 games a year. I was also very interested in getting involved in the international scene."

That was not looking too likely with Australia, even though he had appeared for the Under-23 team. "I did not feel there was much prospect of becoming a full Socceroo. I was not playing regular football and even those that do play in the A-League, not that many of them get selected for the national team."

So there was a chance to take Malaysian citizenship and then, perhaps, play for the national team. You hear stories of the home country in this equation asking players not to do so, or perhaps giving them a full international cap so they are unable to make the switch, but this was not the case for Davies.

"There was no reaction in Australia about my heritage and when I said this is what I am doing, people were surprised, but there was no attempt by FFA to get me to stay. I was getting called up for U-23 games here and there, but they didn't try to talk me out of it."

The chance to go to Pahang, a big club in Malaysia and Southeast Asia, was there. With all due respect to Perth, the passion for the beautiful game is considerably deeper and fiercer on the east coast of Malaysia than the west coast of Australia. It was an attractive prospect.

There was an obstacle, however. If he wanted to play for Pahang then he would have to do so as a Malaysian. Clubs in the Super League are limited to signing four foreign players in their squads, so they like to sign those who can make a difference in positions where they are relatively weak. These positions would usually be strikers, with room also for central defenders and creative midfielders. A club would be reluctant to use one of its precious spots to sign a foreign right-back, as there are plenty of domestic players who can play well in that position.

"That [joining as a Malaysian] was the only option for me," said Davies. "There isn't another way you can come over here as a right-back as a foreign player. It just doesn't happen like that. I wanted to play for the national team and play as a local player, and this was the only way."

It was not entirely simple. Getting a Malaysian passport means that you have to exchange your original. "While Australia allows it, Malaysia doesn't recognise dual citizenship and I had to give up my Aussie passport. It was part of the sacrifice that I have made to get here."

Sacrifice is the key word. Davies has shown a desire to play for Malaysia that is truly impressive and perhaps not one that is shared by all of his international teammates.

"It was strange to give up my Aussie passport. It is strange to go home and then line-up at the passport gate. When I go back to Australia now, I go back as a foreigner. But it is something that I knew would happen when I came here. I was proud to become Malaysian. It felt strange and at the same time, I can look back and say that I made the right decision. I am enjoying my time over here but, as I said, at the time it was strange."

It quickly became less so as Davies made his presence felt on the pitch, taking to his new home with gusto. "Over the last three years, I have had enjoyable seasons at Pahang and captaining the team. In the first year, I won the best young player award in the league and now I play for the national team. Just the sheer amount of games that I have played has been the difference. I have had international exposure that I would probably not have had if I had stayed in Australia."

Also strange, but it is the same for any player, is joining up with a new set of teammates in a new country. "They were very welcoming and there was no animosity, at least as far as I could see. You do hear of people going and the locals being suspicious of the new players coming to take their place, but it was never mentioned. We got on well from the beginning."

It helped that he was playing every week. To make the situation even better, Davies was enjoying the style of play in the Malaysia Super League too.

"The type of football here in the MSL is different to Australia. The technicality of the players is quite high over here and I saw that from the very first game. If you sit down and watch a game, it is exciting and it draws so many fans. The games are end-to-end, so many chances. This is a different style from the A-League, which is more organised and possession-based, and teams tend to wait for an opportunity and break down the other team, but it is difficult to do so as the others are so well-organised. Malaysia is more entertaining for the fans to watch and the players to play in."

It is not just about the style of football, either. Malaysia is more of a football country than Australia, which has a competitive and crowded sporting marketplace. Especially on the east coast, there is huge passion for the beautiful game. "In Perth, I was playing in front of 10,000 fans and my first game with Pahang, I think it was a quarter-final against Kelantan. The stadium was packed about three hours before kick-off and the days before, fans had been camping out trying to get tickets. There was a real buzz around the place, around everywhere. It was the kind of thing I had never experienced in Perth."

But the national team is something else entirely. He had barely started playing for Pahang when there were calls for the national team coach to select this new right-back, who was Malaysian but had come through the Australian youth system. His debut came at the Under-23 level at the 2015 Southeast Asian Games, though it was not a memorable occasion for the Malaysia team, as they failed to get out of the group stage.

Eventually, the call to the senior side came as Malaysia looked to restore its confidence and standing after a 10-0 thrashing by the United Arab Emirates in qualification for the 2018 World Cup. There had also been two 6-0 defeats at the hands of Palestine. New coach Ong Kim Swee may have been drafted in to replace Dollah Salleh on a temporary basis, but he wanted to keep the job.

There had been speculation that Davies would get the call. The player was thrilled, though he did not want to get too excited in case it did not happen. Interestingly, in Malaysia, players who are called for the national team usually find out at the same time as everyone else. "Generally, I find out through social media. If you are connected then that is the first place that it is mentioned and then a day or two later, someone from the club gives you an official document or form that gives you the information you need."

The time was September 2015, the location the Shah Alam Stadium in Selangor. The opposition was Saudi Arabia, a team led by Bert van Marwijk, the coach who had taken his native Netherlands all the way to the final of the 2010 World Cup, only to be defeated by a Spanish goal in extra-time in Soweto. It was quite an introduction to international football in Asia for both Dutchman and new Malaysian. The game was called off just before the end, with home fans throwing flares and other objects to signal their displeasure at how the national team was being run. What should have been a 2-1 defeat, a creditable scoreline given some of the recent thrashings, became an official 3-0 win to the Saudis.

Davies has continued to play for the team since then, and has done so with distinction. "I hadn't watched a lot of Malaysia national team games but I was called up to the national team. It wasn't easy and I made my debut against Saudi Arabia. The family were all proud. Mum and Dad came over and surprised me in my first game. It was eventually abandoned and that was my debut and it was an unusual one. It wasn't a bad result, but we had lost 10-0 in the previous game and the fans were not happy and showed their displeasure towards the end. It was an eventful debut! I think I held my own. I enjoyed it and wanted more. This is what I had been looking to do ever since I started playing football."

His club career has already been something of a roller-coaster. His first campaign with Pahang did not end especially well for the team. The Elephants had been chasing the title but had fallen short to finish second to JDT. A six-point deduction incurred after failing to pay a former player his salary meant a drop to third, which resulted in no AFC Cup the following season. That was a shame, as the club had exited the continental competition at the quarter-final stage in 2015 and was looking to go one or two better the following year. Pahang also failed to capture the FA Cup or the Malaysia Cup. In many ways, it was a fair season, but finishing trophyless is seen as a failure for a number of Malaysian clubs.

There was some personal success, however. At the end of 2015, Davies had been named the Young Player of the Year at the National Football Awards and he flew back from Perth, where he was taking an end of season break, to attend. "That was a real honour for me. I had arrived in Malaysia and nobody knew who I was, yet there I was getting the award. It is nice to be honoured by your peers and it is a prize that I will always treasure."

If anyone thought 2015 was a failure, then 2016 was at a whole different level. Zainal Abidin Hassan left his position as head coach to take over at Selangor. He was replaced by assistant Ahmad Shaharuddin Rosdi. "We knew that it was going to be a big change and that we were losing a well-respected coach, but we also knew that football goes on. Coach Shah knew the players and got on well with them."

For Pahang, 2016 was a year to forget, though it was the first full year in Malaysian football for Davies. It was very different to 2015. Not only did Pahang fail to challenge for the title, they were in the relegation zone for much of the season. In the end, it took an administrative error to keep them up.

On 3 August Pahang lost 1-0 to Kedah, but two months later the victors were found to have fielded an ineligible player, so Pahang were awarded a 3-0 victory. Those three points made the difference between survival and relegation. For a club that was looking to become a private entity and not one bankrolled by the state, it was a close-run thing.

"We were very relieved when we heard the news. This year had been tough and it was great to get something positive to take the pressure off. I think we were starting to play better before that anyway, but it was good to get the three points."

While he still hopes to be a Malaysian international for a long time, Matthew Davies may not be playing his club football in the country. At the moment, Pahang is fine, but this could all change.

"I have always wanted to keep spreading my wings and I do have ambitions to play elsewhere. It would be great to go to Europe, but Japan sounds good too, and even another try in Australia. For me, the important thing is to keep playing well for Pahang and for Malaysia and then who knows where I will end up?"

One thing is for sure. Regardless of what happens in the future, Matthew Davies has no regrets about becoming Malaysian. "I don't really think about what would have happened had I stayed in Australia. Maybe I would be established and played a few games in the A-League, but I am happy where I am now. I made the right decision."

JUNIOR ELDSTÅL
Hello everyone!

That was the title of an open letter penned by Junior Eldstål in July 2013, just a few months after he had arrived in Asia to start playing for Sarawak.

On the pitch he is impossible to miss in the country. At around 190cm (6ft 4in) tall, he towers over almost all teammates and opponents. His time in Malaysia has been a real roller-coaster.

Eldstål was born in Kota Kinabalu but went to Sweden, the homeland of his father, as a toddler and then soon after moved to England. As a youngster he played for some amateur clubs before making the move to Malaysia and Sarawak.

One of the first things he had to do was clear up some confusion about his name and in July 2013, he did just that in an open letter to fans.

First of all, I would like to thank all Malaysians for their support, as it has been immense in the past few months. I only started playing football for

Sarawak in April and the level of encouragement that I have received from
everyone is terrific. Never thought I would make it to the national team
but here I am, and I have to credit that to all the support from fans as well.

However, there are some things I would like to clarify so that all of
us remain on the same page together. My name in the passport is Putera
Nadher Amarhan, and that is undoubtedly my official name in Malaysia
as of now. However, I took my father's name, who has been inspiring to me
since the age of two into my name: Junior Eldstål. I have applied to change
my name here as well, and it is pending approval for now. Thus it would
be brilliant if you guys could refer to me as Junior Eldstål, my family name,
which I am proud of.

Speaking about that, I would also like to mention that I'm actually a
Christian, although my official name may portray that I'm a Muslim. I
have been a Christian all my life and that explains the tattoos on my body.
But at the same time, I have always and will always respect other religions
as well.

Being part of this Malaysian community is a new experience for me,
but it has been nothing short of exhilarating so far. I would like to thank
everyone, including Scott Ollerenshaw, who got me the opportunity to play
here, and of course Robert Alberts and Sarawak FA who took a chance on
me when no one else would. Similarly, I would like to thank all the fans for
their support and I will continue to give 100 per cent in my football career.

Cheers everyone

By the time I talked to Junior, he had already been in Malaysia for four
years and had quite a story to tell.

"As a child, I had rarely gone back to Malaysia, only occasionally
for family events such as weddings," he said. "I have a lot of family in
Europe, which made the long flight to Malaysia less necessary. We spoke
English at home but I had to learn Swedish and Malay phrases, too. My
mother used to always cook me Malaysian dishes now and then growing
up, and made sure I learnt about the culture I was from. I embraced all
the countries and wanted to learn a lot about all of them. It makes your
life more interesting and you feel more at one with other people across
the world."

As well as growing up in more than one country, Eldstål was proficient
in more than one sport. And like quite a few football players before him,
he could probably have earned a living playing on another field.

"Growing up I was very sporty and my father ensured I was always out doing activities and not sitting at home. Of course, only after my homework was done! I actually grew up playing football, basketball and tennis. Tennis was the number one sport at that time. I played at a few private clubs and really loved the game. I started [playing football] at the age of around five or six, where I joined a local team where my friend's dad was a coach."

Becoming a football player was not a given. Had he stayed in England then there is a good chance that it would never have happened. Perhaps, since he has also started his own fashion company, he would be working in that field full-time.

"With professional football in England, there is that famous saying 'Could have, should have, would have...' I made a lot of choices back playing in England because I felt they were right at that time. I had numerous trials and I always played at a good level but the competition in England, as everyone knows, is very big."

It certainly is. As he grew older, then professional football started to look ever more distant, but Eldstål did not see that as a problem at the time.

"I started to fall out of love with the sport and became interested in a lot of other things. Lucky for me I was then enrolled at an academy after a successful trial, as part of taking a degree at Hartpury College. Their facilities were what you would expect at any English Premier League side—we had four pitches, all beautifully cut, and top staff ranging from coaches, nutritionists, analysts, etc, working with us every day to make us better. This really kick-started my career and it was from there I ended up in Malaysia.

"I actually realised that I could play there after doing a work experience trip to Borneo one summer. My close family friend Scott Ollerenshaw kindly let me and my friend come out for the summer to work with him. It was the first time I had been back in Malaysia after six years, so it was very exciting. I loved every minute of it and Scott even managed to get us involved in playing futsal a few days a week in Kota Kinabalu. It was from there I had a phone call a few months later and into my second year of the academy about coming over for a trial at Sarawak and the endless opportunities I would have playing over here in Malaysia. I was overwhelmed but excited. At that point in my life I had fallen in love with Malaysia again and thought, why not?

"Obviously we did not really know what would come of it at the time, so it was all pretty new and exciting for me and my family. They were very supportive and it was nice for them to see me chasing my dream. Sarawak was beautiful and felt very rural. There were no big buildings and busy roads, it was peaceful and the people were very friendly and made me feel welcome immediately. At that time Sarawak played under a full house, the stadium would be filled with red, and it was surreal to be playing in front of 35,000 fans! I loved every minute of it and to top it off we were successful at the time I was there. The fans at the club at that time were amazing. They would fill the stadium at home and, most importantly, away! We had great support, which is one of the main reasons for our undefeated 2013 league campaign and our big run in the Malaysia Cup.

"The players were very friendly. You know what people are like from Borneo with their fellow Borneo brothers! Ronny Harun, Bobby Gonzales and Mafry Balang made me feel the most at home."

His time at Sarawak was going well, but when the call came from Johor Darul Ta'zim, it was hard to resist.

"It was a great feeling to join JDT under TMJ and Bojan Hodak at that time. I already had a great relationship with Bojan who was previously at Kelantan, so the contract and move was made easy. I remember trying to explain it to my friends. It felt like I was joining the Real Madrid of Malaysian football. The facilities, stadium, expectations and so on. The club has many targets, which I love about being here, and to win the league consecutively [in 2015 and 2016] feels amazing. To be a part of a championship-winning side, and better yet going undefeated the season after. Winning two leagues in Malaysia without losing, I think, makes me the first player in Malaysia to do it with two teams!"

There was also the triumph in the 2015 AFC Cup when JDT became the first club in the history of Southeast Asian football to win a continental trophy. Lifting the Asian version of the Europa League was a big deal.

"Playing for such a big club comes with big expectations, but the AFC Cup was different. We were the underdogs, being a club from Malaysia that was on the rise. It was an amazing feeling, but even better than winning the cup was creating history with a great group."

JDT could hold their own in England, believes one of the few people with experience in playing in both countries. "Compared to England, I found the football less physical, and you have a lot more time on the ball in Malaysia. You also have to be much more technical over here as the locals are very gifted technically and you're playing with top imports from around the world, which gives you that experience to take on to where ever you are.

"I would happily say that if our team was playing in England then we could match teams from League One [England's third tier] and even some in the Championship [the second tier]. The only thing that is missing obviously is the physical element. You have a lot of bullies in England who will just play to hurt you, but technically the way we like to play can easily match most clubs back home."

That sort of topic is always going to provoke debate. What is harder to question is the passion that exists in both Malaysia and England.

"In general the love for football here is great. The feeling of playing at the Larkin Stadium is a different level, as is the expectation. To me it only makes me play better, as I want to try my best for the team every time I step across that white line."

So much has happened since Eldstål's 2013 Malaysian debut and the defender has achieved so much. The highlights reel is long.

"In club football, the best moment has to be my first season in Malaysia with Sarawak, gaining promotion and winning the league undefeated. It was my first real triumph out here and it kick-started me to going on to what I have won now. I have won an impressive Premier League title, two Super League titles, two Charity Shields, AFC Cup, FA Cup and the Merdeka Cup. I am still yet to win the Malaysia Cup domestically, and I want to target helping JDT reach the Asia Champions League in the future. I love this game and come from a very humble family. What Malaysia, JDT and Sarawak have done for my career I could not thank them enough. Just know that my love for the game will never change."

For the player, getting the international call-up was an emotional moment. "I remember being on holiday at the time," said Eldstål. "I had a phone call from coach Ong Kim Swee about joining the Under-23s in the University Games and I was so overwhelmed and happy."

It didn't last long. "Twenty minutes later I got another phone call saying it couldn't happen as they registered me too late, so it was a bit of an anti-climax. We then flew back from holiday and received a phone call from Rajagopal asking me to join the squad to Japan and then to play Chelsea and Barcelona. I had only been in Malaysia three months and had obviously made a big impression. I broke down and phoned my dad and mum straight away in tears of joy. To be able to play against clubs I had watched growing up—and even against my friend, who was at that time playing for Chelsea."

While settling in at Sarawak had been smoother than the perfect *teh tarik*, it was not quite the case with the national team. "Personally I found it a lot harder to adapt with the national team. I still could not speak Malay at that time and it was hard not knowing anybody and joining a team where they had been playing together. I had a room to myself for three weeks and was on the phone to Scott weekly asking for advice."

One issue was that the defender, like many who grew up in Europe, is vocal on the pitch. In many parts of Asia, the players are noticeably quieter. For those already in the team, to have a new player arrive who turns on the volume may take quite a bit of getting used to.

"I think it was more how loud I was on the pitch and vocal—other players did not know how to react to it and maybe felt like I was over-vocal. Rajagopal actually held a meeting to say he liked how vocal I was and that players should not be negative and actually embrace it for the team. It was only after three games in that I started to feel more of a bond with my teammates, and that was once Reuben from ATM [Persatuan Bola Sepak Angkatan Tentera Malaysia, the Malaysian Armed Forces team], at the time, had joined the camp and became my 'roomie'. I had guidance with the other boys, too. So I thank him for that."

In terms of passion and pride in turning out for Malaysia, Junior is just as demonstrative. "I get goosebumps every time I hear the national anthem. Some fans may have noticed that I do not sing the song, but that is not because I am not patriotic. Remember, I am from two other backgrounds, England and Sweden, and see them as my first country too. So it's hard for me to be biased towards one. But to represent the Malaysian country is a huge honour.

"My best moment has to be scoring the final goal under Ong Kim Swee in the Merdeka Cup final. I'd previously had two goals disallowed in the group stage and hit the post and bar! So when I scored that goal in front of a crowd of nearly 55,000 it was the best feeling to this day in my career! My worst memory, easily, is being part of that heavy defeat in UAE. That time I was recalled to the side by Dollah Salleh. I felt I was not ready yet, and had long talks with my agent about going. But you learn from things like this and it can only make you become a better player."

That love has been questioned, however. A string of injuries not only interrupted what was becoming a very successful career, it was causing some to doubt his commitment.

"I was diagnosed with two slipped discs, which I have been carrying now for two seasons, hence numerous tears and tendinitis problems. My legs had been compensating for my back, it's been so frustrating, playing three or four games and then having to have a month or so off. But now we know the cause of all the injuries thanks to a specialist in Singapore, and now we can focus on full rehab and making sure that I come back stronger and better. The people that know me know how hard I work off the pitch, so it is only a matter of time until I am back doing what I love. I will keep working hard and fighting off any injury until my body says no—until then, there is no end."

DARREN LOK

At the start of 2016, Darren Lok—an unassuming and pleasant fellow—was playing football for Eastbourne Borough, in the sixth tier of English football and quite unaware of the fuss he was about to make. The striker was there, minding his own business and then he received a Malaysian passport—after quite a wait. It wasn't just a document that provided entry to a different country, it also opened a portal to a different world. He must have wondered exactly what he had let himself in for. Having a Malaysian parent was not going to be preparation for this.

It all started on 23 September as he took possession of the passport. Immediately, he then signed for Johor Darul Ta'zim (JDT) II, the second team of the Malaysian champions that plays in the country's second tier. On 27 September, Lok was selected by national team coach Ong Kim Swee to join a training camp ahead of October's friendly games with Singapore and Afghanistan. These were warm-ups for the 2016 AFF Suzuki Cup that was to kick-off in November.

That's pretty good going—in the space of four days, Lok went from England's sixth division to Malaysia's second, then received an international call-up to play in Singapore's National Stadium, a 55,000-seater state-of-the-art arena.

"It has been a whirlwind few weeks," the player told me in the bowels of that stadium after coming on as a second-half substitute in the 0-0 draw. "I am just happy to be here and ready to start my new career. The standard seemed pretty good but I think after some time to adapt, I will be OK."

There was more. Two days after receiving the summons, the striker was ordered to return back to his club. This was all part of an ongoing feud between JDT and Harimau Malaya, which saw four of the club's internationals, including captain and best player Safiq Rahim, "retire" from the national team. Relations between the club and FAM were frosty to say the least, and this was a problem as JDT have been one of the best clubs in Southeast Asia for the last few years.

Swapping the sixth tier of English football for the international game may sound glamorous, but things are never that simple in Malaysia. Lok and two other JDT II players were told to withdraw from the training camp. He was then allowed to join up with the national team on 3 October as it was an official FIFA match day. There was also some criticism of coach Ong Kim Swee for selecting a player so quickly.

"If we do not call up Darren now, then we will never get a chance to test him in international matches," Ong said. "Those, if there are any, who are unhappy, will have to prove themselves in the league. At the end of the day, priority is getting the best talents for international matches, and not individual interest."

Lok made his debut in that match against Singapore. I saw him after the game, and he was delighted just to be there. It was the same when he was selected for the AFF Suzuki Cup and was played as a late substitute. He was not helped by the fact that this fairly inexperienced team struggled in the opening game against Cambodia, needing a couple of late goals to win 3-2. Then came narrow losses against Vietnam, and painfully, Myanmar. Once again, Lok came on as a substitute.

He was then criticised by well-known Malaysian television pundit "Shebby" Singh—who made a name for himself overseas during an ill-fated spell as the global advisor of Blackburn Rovers—on Fox Sports Television.

"You cannot play in a borough [I think Singh is referring to the name of his former club and perhaps getting it confused with a certain standard of football] and think you are going to play international football," said Singh. "Do not insult Southeast Asia. And that is one question Ong Kim Swee has to answer: on what basis did he pick Darren Lok? On the basis of 45 minutes in the Premier League [Malaysia's second tier]. It's a joke."

These comments prompted an angry article posted on *The Fourth Official*, a lively, informative and opinionated Malaysian sports website, by the player's agent Scott Ollerenshaw, a former Australian international who used to play in Malaysia.

"I have always been uncomfortable with an individual who had a decent career in Malaysia sitting 20 metres behind the centre-back, playing as a sweeper and barking instructions, launching scathing attacks on world class players and coaches who are plying their trade in one of the world's best leagues. How can you critique players and coaches so aggressively when you were not good enough yourself to play at that level? You are not qualified to be a coach because you don't have your badges. You have made a career with your BIG mouth, not unlike your career as a player."

Both seemed to have a point. Lok had been called up quickly and has been playing in the sixth tier of English football. While there is sure to be undiscovered talent in that league, it shows the limited options in Malaysia. Singh had the right to question the call-up, though it is not the fault of the player. Ollerenshaw was stepping in to protect his client. Whether it was necessary or not is debatable, but it was certainly understandable.

So, to sum up: Lok went from the sixth tier of English football, obtained a Malaysian passport, signed for a Malaysian club, got called up to the national team, got withdrawn as part of a spat between the biggest club in the country and the national team, made his debut, and was criticised live on television, causing a national slanging match between two well-known former players. This happened in the space of a few weeks.

This is Malaysian football in a nutshell, all told through the prism of an unwitting striker who had been quietly plugging away in the lower leagues of England and minding his own business. Soon after that, he picked up an injury and missed the first part of the season.

BRENDAN GAN

Brendan Gan, or to give the Australian-born midfielder his full name, Brendan Gan Seng Ling, is now one of Malaysia's best midfielders. He was certainly missed at the 2016 AFF Suzuki Cup due to injury. Perhaps if the former Sydney FC star had not been injured then it would all have turned out very differently for Harimau Malaya.

Gan had been a highly-rated youngster Down Under, making waves for National Premier League team Sutherland Sharks, the suburb of Sydney where he was born. In 2008, he was offered a deal with the youth team of Sydney FC, one of the leading lights of the A-League.

Sydney's youth team turned out to be very competitive indeed, sweeping all before them. That earned Gan the opportunity he really wanted, a chance with the senior side. As is often the case in such situations when results started to go south, the coach John Kosmina started to look for alternatives, a spark to pick things up.

Gan got the nod in November 2008. "This is why I'm here," he said at the time. "I want to play first grade, A-League and [I'm] pretty happy that I got the call up. It's going to be a big game and hopefully I can make an impact." This is why such players are valuable in Malaysia. Gan had the football education and had to first survive and then prosper in a tough and competitive environment.

He certainly did not look out of place at the pinnacle of Australian football. He came off the bench for his debut against Central Coast Mariners for a five-minute introduction. Just a few days later, he came on again and this time scored the winning goal for Sydney against Newcastle Jets. It was the club's first victory in seven games. Soon after he was making his first start. In his second, he opened the scoring in a 3-1 win over Wellington Phoenix.

The departure of Kosmina as coach early in 2009 was a turning point. His replacement was Vitezslav Lavicka, a tactician from the Czech Republic, who was not such a big fan of the youngster. In November 2010, Gan started talking about Malaysia. "My inbox [on] Facebook is overflowing with messages from Malaysian fans who want me to come and play for them," he said. "There's been no contact so far from the Malaysian FA but I'd definitely be open to it."

In 2011 he was off to Sabah, the most easterly state in Malaysia. Kota Kinabalu is a two-hour flight from Kuala Lumpur, but it marked the start of his Malaysian adventure. He was registered as a foreign player despite his Malaysian heritage. There had been talk in the media about the possibility of playing for the Tigers. The Australian national team is obviously stronger, but much harder to break into. If, as a player, you are being released by A-League clubs, then an international call-up is not going to happen any time soon. Even so, Gan's experience and determination to keep looking for a route to the top stood in contrast to many of those in Malaysia, who, Balestier coach and former Kelantan player Marko Kraljevic told me, lack hunger.

"They enjoy life in Kota Bharu," said Kraljevic. "It is beautiful but you need to focus on the game and do good training. I did extra training by myself, as the training was not good enough. I was usually the only one. Now things are changing but the coach often only focuses on the team and as individuals we never improved, there was never much attempt to improve the players. Beckham was not a great crosser by accident. He trained every day. Technically, the players were good but they never worked to push to the next level."

Kraljevic had grown up in Yugoslavia, working hard and dreaming of playing for and against the elite of European football. "We always dreamed. We looked at AC Milan with Gullit, Van Basten and Rijkaard and we wanted to play there, we wanted to play against Bayern Munich. Before that was Liverpool and Dalglish, and this was always our dream. The bar we set was very high, we wanted to achieve something."

This was not the case in Malaysia and Singapore. "There was no next level and I don't why. Maybe they are too happy with what they have. They don't want to move to Korea or Japan, which is the next level for them and after that, they can move to Europe. This is a problem still today. Here at Balestier, I tell my players that if you don't think you can play for the national team then your place is not here and you can go away. If you just come because of your contract and you have to come and that you do so without a goal, without a desire to push yourself. All players should push the bar higher."

That is what Gan was doing. He left no stone unturned in his desire to become as good as he could be. It made him battle-hardened, tough and ambitious. Then came the inquiry from Sabah, as he recounted to *FourFourTwo*.

"I was immediately tempted when I searched online about the place. I had previously visited the country a few times to see my grandmother and relatives in Negeri Sembilan, but Sabah looked totally different and amazing. In fact, it looked a lot like my home, as I lived by the beach. I had never left Australia for an extended period of time prior to that, but I thought it [a place with a similar geography] would be a great opportunity to broaden my horizon."

Sabah FA was a tough introduction to life in the beautiful homeland of his father. The Rhinos were just not cut out for life in the top flight and there were some painful lessons and defeats. Being mauled 9-0 by LionsXII sticks in the memory, despite the best attempt of fans to forget, and the 6-3 loss to Terengganu also hurt. Relegation was inevitable, and so was the players not being offered new contracts. Foreign players tend not to last too long, even those with Malaysian fathers.

"My move was based on trying to get some game time and experience at a high level," he said. "It was a great experience. I didn't know much of the language. The standard of football is different, and they rely on the passing game."

There was then a return to Australia in 2013 for a season in the NSW Premier League with Rockdale City Suns FC, before the big move came. That was to Kelantan in 2014. If Sabah was struggling, then Kelantan were far from it as one of the biggest teams, not only in Malaysia, but the whole of Southeast Asia.

Playing for the 2012 champions and now a Malaysian citizen, both the fans and Gan waited for what was expected to be his first call-up, an August friendly against Tajikistan. This was also the first game in charge for new coach Dollah Salleh. The former Pahang boss and Malaysia legend was preparing to defend the country's title at the 2014 AFF Suzuki Cup.

Gan, however, was not included in the squad and did not even make the standby list. "I was not necessarily disappointed that I did not get called up because I understand and respect the decision made by Dollah Salleh. I have only been here for a few months, so I do not expect to easily slot into the national team. The national call-up will come if I manage to prove myself and, most importantly, play at my best for Kelantan."

"I am still proud of who I am and where I came from, but I am here because I want to be part of the future and help Malaysian football grow," he says. "I was lucky to be part of the A-League's rise to prominence and I believe that Malaysia is exactly at that same spot right now. Right now, the Super League is very close to emulating the A-League. The following in Malaysia is massive compared to in Australia and we have fantastic players. So, who is to say that Malaysia cannot achieve what Australia did in years to come?"

Meanwhile, he was getting closer to representing his country. Gan was called into the preliminary squad for the 2014 Suzuki Cup but did not make the cut for the final 22-man list. He appeared as an average player for the U-23 team. But it was surely going to happen in 2015 as it was all going quite well up in the northeast, until injury struck in the opening game of the Malaysia Super League season. Gan tore his anterior cruciate ligament (ACL) in his right knee and was carried off the pitch five minutes into the second half.

It was a devastating blow and pictures of the player in tears at the side of the pitch were seen by all fans. Coach George Boateng tweeted:

"It's heartbreaking to lose a quality player like Brendan Gan. He will be hugely missed. We wish you a speedy recovery."

He had to wait until March 2016 for a first call up, and it came against Saudi Arabia. After some terrible results in qualification for the 2018 World Cup with a 10-0 thrashing handed out by the United Arab Emirates and two 6-0 losses to Palestine, few were looking forward to the trip to Jeddah to take on a talented team coached by Bert van Marwijk.

Yet Malaysia held the hosts to a creditable 2-1 scoreline, with Gan impressing. Now he could look forward to the AFF Suzuki Cup, to be held later that year. Yet disaster struck again. Playing for the national team in a friendly in Indonesia in September, he was carried off after rupturing the ACL in his left knee.

"No athlete is truly tested until they stare an injury in the face and come out on the other side stronger. I've done it once now and came out stronger from it ..." The attitude shown by the player was truly impressive. Nobody can accuse Brendan Gan of lacking fight, confidence, ambition or a determination to improve.

PLAYING SINGAPORE

While Matthew Davies is now a regular in the Malaysia national team, he did not appear in the friendly against Singapore in October 2016 after falling ill a few days before. He watched, wistfully, on television, wishing he was at the National Stadium, helping his country defeat its greatest rival.

"I think it is difficult not to get caught up in all the hype surrounding the game with Singapore. It is built up a fair bit, but I don't feel anything against them. There is a lot of feeling around the game but the players don't sit down and tell each other that 'this is a game we have to win'. That's not the way it works, but I am sure there would be some special feeling if we had won. For Malaysian fans and players, there is nothing better than beating Singapore. Of course, that means there is nothing worse than losing against them!"

Davies is aware of the difference between the two rivals when it comes to naturalising players. He prefers the Malaysian version. "My opinion is that you should have some type of connection with the country. I see a lot of players who go to Hong Kong and Singapore and play there for five years and then go and get naturalised and then they are happy about having an Asian passport. There should be some kind of link. It should be a parent or another relative, but there should be something that gives you that special feeling about the team you are playing for."

The defender says that having two nationalities does not weaken your feelings for either country—it is possible to feel patriotic about both.

"The feeling you have is not diluted when you have two nationalities. You can equally have respect for each country and I feel that. I grew up in Australia with my Malaysian background and it has kind of switched now. Malaysia has given me everything and that is something I will never forget and will always appreciate, but there is also the childhood I had in Australia."

For this player, more than Singapore, facing Australia while wearing the famous yellow-and-black stripes would provoke special and unique feelings. "It would be strange, and I admit that I have gone over that in my head a few times. I think I would sing both anthems! I think that I would also build it up. I feel like I would have a point to prove against Australia and I would be definitely trying a little harder."

With all the qualification games coming up over the next few years for future Asian and World Cups, it could happen, and there is always a possibility of a friendly or two. "There is a good chance. I am young and I hope to be playing international football for many years to come, so there will be opportunities."

Eldstål works just over the border from Singapore. "Every Malaysian player knows that Singapore are the one team you have to beat. Games against them are special and losing is not really an option. People talk about it for a long time before and after. It is good to have rivals and Singapore are good rivals for Malaysia and vice versa. I just hope that both teams can become two of the best in Asia."

Zainal Abidin Hassan used to play against Singapore when the Lions were in the Malaysia Cup. "I always enjoyed playing Singapore. There was a special feeling. We wanted to beat them and they always wanted to beat us. Selangor and Singapore, we had a great rivalry. These were the games that you looked forward to. The SEA Games final in 1989 stands out. There was a great atmosphere in the stadium on that day and to win the gold against our old rivals was a very nice feeling."

CHAPTER 9

FEDERATION REVOLUTION?

Malaysia and Singapore fans never agree on which national team is better and which federation is worse.

—Singapore fan at Singapore Sports Hub, October 2016

Albert Camus was once asked by his friend Charles Poncet which he liked more: football or the theatre. The story goes that the French philosopher replied: "Football, without hesitation." Camus was a goalkeeper and had played for the junior team of Racing Universitaire Algerios (RUA). According to reports and those who watched him between the sticks, he was a decent player before he was struck down by tuberculosis.

When, in his fifties, he was asked to write about his spell with RUA for a magazine, he came up with the following quote: "After many years during which I saw many things, what I know most surely about morality and the duty of man I owe to sport and learned it in the RUA."

The Albert Camus society gets asked about this fairly often and this is their regular response. "People have read more into these words than, perhaps, Camus would want them to. He was referring to a kind of simple morality he wrote about in his early essays, an ethic of sticking up for your friends, of valuing courage and fair play. Camus believed that the people of politics and religion try to confuse us with convoluted moral systems to make things appear more complicated than they really are, possibly to suit their own agendas. People may do better to look to the simple morality of the football field than to politicians and philosophers."

They may indeed. Football is a simple game made complicated by the goings-on that surround it. The beautiful game may be beautiful, but some of the people it attracts are anything but.

There are plenty of examples all over the world of those who run the game, not for fans, or for the sport, but for their own ends. The popularity of football, the power it has and the money it attracts is both a blessing and a curse.

I heard it said once that fans get the federation they deserve. It's not true. The politicians—well some of them at least—get involved and take advantage of the passion, the dreams and the hopes of millions, and enjoy it all a little too much. In some parts of Asia, it seems as if the more passionate and football-loving the country is, the worse the federation is. In Malaysia and Singapore, the two federations are more involved than most. There are few—if any—federations around the world that are universally popular among fans but in the elite countries of Europe, those that run the game are not part of the everyday conversation in a way that they are in Malaysia and Singapore. Pick up a newspaper in London or Berlin and you can go for days without seeing the FA or DFB mentioned at all. Try doing that in Kuala Lumpur or Singapore and you have more chance of finding satay that can measure up to that first satay you had on your first visit to the country (don't ask me why that is, it just is).

But then there are times when the headlines are warranted and you really need to be reading about the goings on at FAM or FAS, two brothers from different mothers.

MALAYSIAN ELECTIONS

Who could have guessed in July 2016, when there was virtual war between the Crown Prince of Johor Tunku Ismail Sultan Ibrahim (TMJ) and FAM, that eight months later he would be in charge of the organisation he criticised with such vehemence? It seemed as likely as Figo leaving Barcelona for Real Madrid in November 1999.

TMJ (short for Tunku Mahkota Johor, or "Crown Prince of Johor") was the man behind the rise of JDT (Johor Darul Ta'zim), another of the top five most important acronyms in Malaysian football. After taking control of the club in 2013, things changed for the better. The Malaysia Super League title won in 2014 was just the first of a hat-trick thanks to investments that brought many of the best players in the country to the Larkin Stadium, as well as talented foreign stars including, for a while in 2014, Argentine midfielder Pablo Aimar.

While it has been refreshing to see the club, based in Johor Bahru, a city located just on the Malaysian side of the border with Singapore, investing in quality foreign players, there has also been plenty of money spent on facilities and infrastructure. This includes a training ground and complex that will be lit up and visible from Singapore. It is not just the money, but the vision, the hard work, the determination and patience that sets the club apart in Malaysia and the rest of the region. JDT have set the standard for the rest of the country to follow—though for the most part it has not, at least not yet. That led TMJ to be vocal about the failings of the other clubs, especially the most important: the Football Association of Malaysia.

TMJ has been a long-standing critic of the organisation and also of coach Ong Kim Swee, who took the job in late 2014 after a number of thrashings suffered by the national team (with a 10-0 loss to the United Arab Emirates just the worst of a bad bunch).

After a tour of Oceania in June 2016—and more indifferent results—TMJ blasted the national team's training methods and schedule and accused the FAM of corruption and mismanagement. "You don't need to show me and the current generation that you as old-timers are struggling to accept that the world and time has changed," he said.

This was manna from heaven for headline writers, who could just sit back and enjoy the show. Fans loved it, too. Here was a high-profile and powerful football person (and also royalty) saying the things that they were saying to their friends over *teh tarik*, but doing it with such devastating effect.

What followed were some serious accusations against those who had been in charge of running the game for decades. "What's strange is that after all these years, all of you can accept and stand the 30 years of corruption within FAM." He said he had in his possession a pen drive that was evidence of all kinds of wrongdoing and corruption at FAM going back a very long time indeed.

"[It contains] information and activities within the FAM, the media personnel that the FAM always use, including former footballers in Malaysia, the amount of money taken by FMLLP (the body that runs the league) and given to the FAM, as well as a rubbish auditor's report given to me by my high-ranking friends in Kuala Lumpur. Maybe it's time for football supporters of this country to see the truth and judge for themselves."

It was explosive stuff but there was more. Around the same time that all this was going on, four JDT players announced their retirement from the national team. These were Aidil Zafuan Abdul Radzak, S. Kunanlan, Amirul Hadi Zainal and, the most damaging, captain, 2014 Suzuki Cup top scorer and star midfielder Safiq Rahim.

"The time has come for me to retire from the national team and give opportunities to other players to carry on my roles," wrote Safiq on Facebook. "The achievements accomplished, such as helping the Under-23 national team win gold at the 2009 SEA Games and becoming the 2010 AFF Suzuki Cup [champions] with the senior team will surely inspire the next generation of footballers to give more positive results to the country."

The reasoning behind the retirements was, so sources said, the players being unhappy at the training methods and the lack of intensive training sessions. These were important members of the national team, and it was not like Malaysia could afford to lose them. Safiq was the best player in the country and one of the best in the region.

It was obviously big news, but it was also just another salvo in the war between the country's biggest and best club and the national federation.

"It is easy to criticise them," said TMJ in a statement regarding the retirement of the "JDT Four". "But you have to put yourself in their shoes to understand their decision. These players love their country. Representing the country is the greatest honour they've ever had in their careers. They don't do this because they don't love Malaysia. They do this because they are human beings like you and me. They do this because they are tired of unnecessary call-ups [where] they have to spend months in training camps doing nothing. They have to play for an organisation that never stands up for their well-being, and they don't even do anything when their compatriots don't receive salaries from their respective clubs."

While it was upsetting to read such an important figure in Malaysian football say such things about how the national team was set-up and organised, it was also refreshing and significant at the same time. For once, the big issues were being discussed out in the open—because when the crown prince of Johor speaks in such terms, it can't be ignored.

He went on, claiming that Tengku Abdullah Sultan Ahmad Shah, the president of FAM, never attended training or meetings and didn't know the players' names or even the fact they existed at all. TMJ added that there were other players who also wanted to follow in the footsteps of the now infamous four but were too scared to do so.

"... But as usual, FAM does what they do best which is ignoring them, just like how they have ignored clubs and football fans across the country. You should stand for the players, clubs and other organisations and demand changes in FAM. Whether they like it or not, one day they have to change."

It is hard to think of any country in the world that has seen the famous CEO of a club attack a national association so passionately and seriously. Alex Ferguson was often happy to give his opinion of the English FA when in charge of Manchester United, but it wasn't like this. This was relentless.

FAM had been receiving punch after punch and was on the ropes. It was in a difficult position as, firstly, many fans were quite happy to see it getting savaged; and secondly, it wanted to defend itself but without making the situation worse.

"It was both shocking and unsurprising," said a source at FAM who preferred not to be named. "On the one hand, we could not believe that such a major figure was saying such things in public and in such a way. It had everyone running around in circles. But on the other hand, there was a feeling that something was building with TMJ, that sooner or later there was going to be some kind of showdown or argument, or whatever you want to call it. It was actually a good thing for FAM—well, I can say that looking back but at the time, nobody knew what to do."

After a few days, Secretary-General Datuk Hamidin Mohd Amin held a press conference, refuting most of the claims and dealing with the issue of retirements. "We didn't receive any notice from any of them. If they want to quit the national team, so be it. But they must do so in the correct manner." Hamidin added: "Not one player has complained about training but we will speak to them…maybe some are not satisfied."

Coach Ong was visibly upset with TMJ's comments that the players were unhappy with his training methods and that there was a lack of intensity. The coach had been put in a difficult position. Results had not been great, but that had been the case for some time and it can't have been easy to see his training methods dragged out into the open like this.

"We were all waiting to see what TMJ would do," said the source. "We had no idea how it would play out. People criticised FAM all the time, but always the situation solved itself or it just got forgotten and life carried on—but this was different."

Amid great ceremony in August, TMJ handed the pen drive to the Youth and Sports Minister Khairy Jamaluddin. The minister also criticised FAM for frantically trying to find the person who had provided the information on the pen drive rather than allowing it go public. A few days later, the Malaysian Anti-Corruption Commission cleared FAM of any wrongdoing. But tensions remained between all parties.

That was not, however, the end of the story. The following March there was to be an election for a new president, one that had been brought forward as the incumbent, Tengku Abdullah, wanted to step down to focus on other duties—which cynics argued was just an official confirmation of what was already happening.

Speculation was rife that TMJ would try to throw his hat onto the doorknob of the presidential office. Would the organisation's biggest critic step forward to take on the job? Journalists speculated he would and in the end, he did. It was a fine and brave act. The man was already successful in football and had already brought about some change in the country's soccer scene, and nobody would have blamed him if he had ran from the FAM elections as fast as he could. Like all political leaders who know that however popular they may be when they take office, they are almost certain to be unpopular when they leave, the same is true of federation chiefs. Whatever goodwill the boss may have at the start is not going to last forever without positive results. But at least he tried.

"I did not decide to do it because I wanted to, but rather, it's the fear of what will happen should this football institution fall into the wrong hands," said the Crown Prince in February 2017 via Facebook—his use of social media being another aspect that marked him out from the old guard. "If that happens, it will be back to square one. This is our chance to change it forever and bring it to the likes of Japan, Thailand, and all the other successful countries."

There were other candidates expected to challenge. Sports minister Khairy Jamaluddin and former Home Ministry secretary-general Tan Sri Aseh Che Mat abandoned their campaigns on 13 February after TMJ had confirmed his participation.

That left one rival for the most important job in Malaysian football: Tan Sri Annuar Musa, another one of the key figures in the country's football scene. The then president of Kelantan FA had been making news for years. Educated at University College of London, he was erudite, friendly and talked a very good game. And, when TMJ took over at JDT, Kelantan were the leading team in Malaysia after winning the Malaysia Super League title in 2011 and then going two better and taking the treble in 2012. Even in 2013, the Red Warriors won the FA Cup and reached the final of the Malaysia Cup.

Yet Annuar's recent past was not without some major blemishes. There had been concerns at Kelantan. In 2015 and 2016, there were reports of financial issues and the team were struggling to pay coaches and players. Early in 2016, with the situation becoming more serious, a major sponsor was announced.

It raised (immaculately-plucked) eyebrows. The company in question was Vida Beauty, a popular cosmetic company that specialised in whitening cream products. The CEO was a flamboyant businesswoman, Datuk Seri Hasmiza Othman, who had built up a successful empire from scratch. She was to pay 16–20 million ringgit (US$4–5 million) for the privilege of sponsoring not only one of the biggest clubs in Malaysia but one of the biggest in the whole of Southeast Asia.

Such figures meant that the announcement could be glossed over as one of those things that players (and fans) have to buy into. The trademark catchphrase of the company was "Qu Puteh" (which translates roughly as "I am fair"), with the CEO pouting and placing her index finger on her chin. It all looked a bit strange, but when the deal was as significant as this one then you can accept a little strange.

But there was more to worry about. The beauty business guru started to paint the team's Sultan Muhammad IV Stadium pink. The team's nickname, the Red Warriors, became "Qu Puteh Red Warriors". This was all getting a little out of hand and Kelantan were starting to become a laughing stock in Malaysian football—but there was worse to come.

In televised MSL games early in the 2016 season Hasmiza was there, cheekily uttering her catchphrase as soon as the half-time and full-time adverts came on television; worst of all, there she was during games, sitting where the coach should sit on the bench. When she knew the cameras were on her, well, you can guess what she did. Add to the fact that she was often on her phone, wore whatever colours she wanted and came and left the bench area whenever she wanted, it was clear that it was all getting a bit too much.

There was even talk of her getting involved in transfers and she talked of her desire to take over a European club. Football Malaysia Limited Liability Partnership (FMLLP) told her to get off the bench, and given Kelantan's poor results in the early stages, she threatened to take her money and run. "People from all sides are pressuring and blaming me instead for what has happened," she said in April 2016.

"As an entrepreneur, obviously I would want a return on my investment, in whatever form they may be. Especially when this particular investment was not a small one, but in the millions," she argued. "I just want Kelantan to appreciate my sacrifices. The slump in their performance actually also affects my image and product sales."

Her presence, or at least the way it was all handled, affected the image of Kelantan FA and Malaysian football. The worst part of it all was that most of the money does not seem to have been paid—though Vida Beauty claimed that it had been—and halfway through the season the deal was ended. It left the club more in the lurch than ever and the players were growing tired, not of having to wear pinker shirts, but of not receiving the money they were owed.

Jon McKain arrived from Australia at the end of 2014 and took the arrival of the club's new sponsor in his stride.

"I hadn't been here long enough to let it bother me," he told me in October 2016 when he was heading back home Down Under. "I don't think fans were bothered, either. We had plenty of change strips.

"At the start there was massive hype. She is well-known and has money and big plans, but what they promised basically never happened. The club puts a lot of its problems down to promises not being honoured. Even with the issues, Kelantan finished fourth this season. The potential is huge.

"The fans are great. They have passion and a love for football and the team. There is one team in the town and the fans love it. So it is sad to see how let-down the fans have been.

"We have had a good team but changing coaches, sacking foreign players and the ongoing financial issues make it hard. It is hard to focus when you are not getting paid."

It is hard to argue with that. Coach Steve Darby lasted barely six months into a two-year contract that was signed in October 2013. The Englishman is still waiting to receive a fair chunk of the wages he is owed by the club, one that he still talks of in affectionate terms. He wrote me a letter in 2016 describing how he felt about the situation, which he was happy to see shared with a wider audience:

I have been asked, am I angry about the whole Kelantan not paying due amounts on time saga. Anger is the wrong emotion, perhaps frustration and disappointment are better words.

Frustrated in that it took two years, hundreds of emails, legal fees and many unanswered questions to reach a conclusion. A conclusion that may not be over yet, as the final judgment given to me in Bahasa, not English, is still being analyzed for its legality and accuracy of calculation.

Disappointment is also a key word in the way the whole scenario unfolded. I have no problem with the employer's right to terminate an employee. As long as the correct contractual and legal procedures are adhered to. I could argue that being terminated in the semifinal of an FA cup, fourth in a league and just having played a horrendous AFC Cup schedule was unjust. But that is the employer's rights. Though I did find out via my players before I was formally told (in a restaurant at midnight); also it was on Facebook before I was told in person. But if that is the way a club wishes to run its affairs, then so be it.

However, I was offered a position as Technical Director of the club in lieu of head coach. This is a position I had said was much needed by the club and the person who fulfilled it should be fluent in Malay, if not Kelantanese, and have a strong playing and coaching background in the state. I was offered the role then "unofficially" told by an executive high up in the club that the aim was if I took up the position to make my employment so unworkable that I would resign and money would be saved. [This is] a ploy that many clubs are trying to use, particularly against foreign employees. Sometimes it's called "resting" [resting coaches, in the hope that they will resign of their own accord, is not uncommon in Malaysia] even! How embarrassing and degrading, not only for the employee, but the employer. Do they think anyone believes this method of termination is anything but a money-saving scam?

I was initially given a full contractual pay-out by the FAM committee, but when this was appealed against (no problem with that) some of the grounds of appeal were hilarious! Including I had run away from Kelantan. Run away? Leaving the apartment professionally cleaned, the car returned full of petrol and all personal bills paid two weeks after my sacking.

Eventually, after many requests written and verbal by my lawyers and myself, a decision was made by the appeals committee to reduce my payout due to me gaining employment in football after being terminated by Kelantan (I coached in the Indian Super League and as national coach for Laos). However, I never received any information how the financial calculations were made? Also if this is the case, then if I had left my contract with Kelantan on my own volition, then I would only have to be paid compensation until they got a new coach? Which in this case was two hours before I was terminated! The replacement told me himself.

I have no personal problems with Tan Sri Annuar; he was always straight to me and to my face, never behind my back. I used to enjoy our 3am team discussions, but I can honestly say he always left the team selection to me. As another coach who was terminated after me (I think it's four now) spoke, there were "unseen hands" operating in the club. I know this as I understand Bahasa far more than people realised and heard management saying and doing things that were not for the good of the team. I also reported players for unprofessional behaviour (drunkenness) in the correct manner—privately, not in the media, but the players were backed over the coach and staff.

It makes for sobering reading, especially as the tone is one of disappointment rather than anger. A child can handle the anger of a parent but disappointment is a much more serious and harder emotion to shake off, especially when it comes from a man who has spent years coaching all over Southeast Asia and is genuinely well-regarded.

But it was Annuar versus TMJ, and there was no love lost between these two high-profile figures. The media and the fans had what they wanted: the two heavyweights of Malaysian football ready to do battle at the ballot box. Even more exciting was that, although they had worked together in past FAM elections, they did not seem to like each other and there was soon a war of words for journalists to report in breathless fashion.

TMJ warned Annuar, who was also information chief of the ruling party UMNO, not to damage the party.

"The state of Johor is also a stronghold of the ruling party today. The day for people to cast their votes is edging closer, so don't stir up a hornet's nest, because there will be consequences. Tan Sri, don't be a liability to your own party. You clearly have your own interest within the party," he wrote in a Facebook post on the Johor Southern Tigers titled "Mind Your Own Business".

Annuar had earlier told TMJ that if he wanted to lead Malaysian football then he should do so by standing in an election and not by proxy. The retort came back that the Johor man would not take advice on leadership from a man who had failed to lead.

Just before the start of the 2017 season, Annuar had threatened that Kelantan, due to the problems finding sponsors, would not participate in the coming season. "You shouldn't be a captain who abandons his ship at the first sight of trouble. As you've barely managed to run KAFA properly, it's better that you forget about leading Malaysian football," TMJ said.

In the end, just a few days before the vote at FAM was due to take place and with TMJ the favourite to win, Annuar pulled out of the race. "I have decided to show respect to the other candidate, the Johor crown prince, so he can win uncontested and be FAM president," he told reporters in parliament.

"The leadership, which would be elected into office, must have all-round support when they start their jobs."

In the end, all's well that ends well. This was a time to pull together and Annuar, who always seemed to have other political ambitions with which to occupy his time, pulled out. Given the on-going financial struggles of Kelantan, with players still waiting to be paid, it was probably for the best.

Now Malaysian football fans had what they wanted. A young, ambitious, determined and confident football chief with a clear idea of what he wanted to do and the track record to show that he usually delivers on his promises. It should be a very interesting few years.

As well as the merits of football in England and Malaysia, Junior Eldstå* is well-equipped to discuss what it is like to work with TMJ and what fans in Malaysia can expect of the new man in charge of FAM.

"He is the breath of fresh air that Malaysian football needed. After so many years, even before I arrived, there was so much disappointment and I think it was time for a big change. For me he will personally do great and change the way people think about Malaysian football. There is so much talent and opportunity, but with the wrong guidance in the past. Now with the right man behind the team and the country it is only a matter of time until the fans start seeing big changes."

As for Kelantan, the ascension of TMJ to the FAM job brought a wave of reforming energy and in May 2017, the team was docked six points for failing to pay players.

SINGAPOREAN ELECTIONS

If the election at the Football Association of Malaysia ended smoothly—or rather, went so smoothly that there was no contest at all—the same could not be said in Singapore, where the elections made headlines even in the non-football media.

Elections can be dangerous things. Just look at Brexit, Trump and the French presidential race: we are in the era of national elections with a global impact, ones that upset the established order with the voters demanding a departure from the status quo.

In football too, there has been a reaction against the establishment that has run the sport for years, and not always for the benefit of the beautiful game. From the world governing body FIFA to the region that is Southeast Asia, there are new hands at the helm.

In February 2016, a third major football vote in ASEAN occurred in the space of just over 12 months. The long-term and controversial tenure of Worawi Makudi as the boss of Football Association of Thailand was officially ended. Somyot Poompanmoung promised transparency and an end to the corruption scandals of the Worawi years. The former police chief spearheaded a coalition of interests in Thai football—retail giants King Power, most clubs, fans and the government—who wanted change. The jury is still out as to whether he has, or will, deliver, but the message was clear.

In Singapore, the opposing sides seemingly offer the stark contrast that has become the norm in recent elections: more of the same or something quite different. That was obviously the motive behind naming Bill Ng's campaign Team Game Changers. It seemed to be a not so subtle, albeit wise, attempt to align itself with the global zeitgeist.

It was understandable given the nature of the opposition. Team LKT is led by former FAS vice-president Lim Kia Tong. They looked like the establishment, sounded like the establishment and smelled like the establishment.

In the United Kingdom and the United States of late, this has been enough to ensure defeat. Ng's attempt to seize the mantle of the upstart, the outsider and the anti-establishment voice, seemed to make sense—even if, like Donald Trump, it is not completely accurate.

Yet, there have been problems for the Hougang United owner. The campaign went badly. When the self-proclaimed agents of change are being arrested, released on police bail and talking of what happened to $500,000 donations, the situation, at best, does not look good.

Also, real outsiders tend not to win in football. This is not a real democracy and the disaffected masses do not get a vote. The 44 voters casting theirs were a different kind of electorate.

A year earlier in Thailand, the opposition candidate was the head of the Thai police, a position that you do not occupy if you do not have close ties and support from the ruling elite. After years of Worawi Makudi in charge and his supporters still in powerful positions, Somyot needed powerful friends just to get things done.

The new boss in Malaysia is a crown prince. Again, TMJ is not exactly a revolutionary looking to overthrow the *ancien régime* and bring democracy to the masses. But perhaps that is just the way it has to be in Southeast Asian football at the moment.

In Singapore, it was the first election in the body's 125-year history, with all previous holders of office appointed by the government. That very fact ensured that things were going to be different. Two teams of nine people were fighting for control and they were slated to fill various positions on the council, including president and vice-president.

In one corner Team LKT was projecting the idea of a steady pair of hands, business very much as usual. In the other, Ng may have set himself up as the man with a broom to sweep clean, but he had been involved in Singapore football for years.

Ng is the chairman of S-League club Hougang United. Alex Weaver, an English coach who had a short time in charge of the club, described what sounded like a strange experience there. In pre-season, Weaver had started to experiment, playing with ten men in warm-up games to try and give his players practice for the coming season. After explaining that he was going to withdraw a player at half-time, Weaver did just that and his team lost.

According to the coach, he was told by the club that the next pre-season friendly was a must-win. Unsurprisingly, Weaver did not last long. Soon after, he joined Warriors FC and led the team to a very satisfying title.

That could perhaps be dismissed as something that was not much more than a cultural clash. British experience with Ng was not altogether positive, either. He was linked with a takeover of Scottish giants Glasgow Rangers in 2012 before withdrawing his bid. That made headlines in the UK and then in April 2017, he made a lot more in his home country.

Ng was arrested four days before the vote was due to take place.

Always a controversial figure because his clubs' main revenue streams come from legalised gambling, he was released on police bail, as was former FAS president Zainudin Nordin, general secretary Winston Lee and Ng's wife Bonnie Wong.

It was all down to an alleged misuse of funds at Tiong Bahru Football Club, also owned by Ng. Earlier in April, Ng said at a press conference that he had donated $500,000 to FAS and wanted to know where it had gone. He claimed that he did not know what had happened. Lee claimed that Ng had been told exactly where it was going, to the FAS through the ASEAN Football Federation.

It was not looking good for the self-styled new guard. And when the election actually took place on a Saturday morning in late April at the Sports Hub Black Box Auditorium, it was over very quickly. So much so, that the press conference that had been scheduled to be held for the winner to say what he wanted to say was brought forward by 90 minutes.

It went 30-13 in favour of Team LKT. In the end, it was hard to remember what all the excitement was about as it finished so quietly and without fuss. There was a healthy amount of good-natured comments from both loser and victor.

"They deserve it," said Ng, who accepted defeat graciously. "They are the best eleven—the best eleven wins. We will play the twelfth man. Singapore football has to be reunited but not split." After the business with the police, it was probably wise to bow out gracefully.

Lim also sounded a conciliatory note. "I call upon everyone in the football community, the players, coaches, administrators, the volunteers, the media, the fans and even our opponent today—to set aside our past differences and work together for the good of Singapore football. It will take all of us to rejuvenate football for our country."

"History will be the ultimate judge as to what happens from tomorrow onwards," he added.

In that, he is certainly wrong. The judging will come thick and fast, and not from history. It is going to be a big few years for the Football Association of Singapore.

EPILOGUE

One thing is for sure: there is history, vibrancy, heartbreak and delight in Singaporean and Malaysian football. It is not always about being the best, but sometimes the ideal approach is just to enjoy it for what it is.

It is hard, though. It is hard not to look back. And there are some realities that were obviously better in the old days.

For one thing, there needs to be more places to play, as Soh Chin Aun rightly points out. "Right in front of my house when I was eight years old or ten years old, was a nice football pitch, until it was taken out. It is like education. Before you can be an accountant, you need to have a school to study and then you can be an accountant. Without a football field, without a facility, how can we play football, how can we be good?"

There were more heroes, more fans and a greater multicultural representation than nowadays. If football has one power, then it is that of bringing people together. Look back through history and you see famous names such as Chow Chee Keong, Lim Teong Kim and Soh Chin Aun. Yet these days, the lack of Chinese players in Malaysian and Singapore football is apparent.

Penang president Zairil Khir Johari told me that Malaysian football was becoming less multicultural: "It's a shame. In the nineties, every team would have a mixture of Chinese, Malay and Indians. Now there are hardly any Chinese players in the league. It is a combination of things. You can't say that football does not pay well any more. It does, and it pays too much. Now I am in the thick of it, I see we are paying too much for the quality we are getting. That distorts football in Malaysia. Maybe it starts from grassroots, maybe people want different things for their kids and people are better off and don't think about football as a career for your kids but in the past, people were more working class."

It seems that the job of football player is not something that many Singaporean parents find appealing for their children. This is a cultural situation that is not easy to change. It was the same when Jan Poulsen arrived at the end of the 1990s.

"I soon found that the culture was different than Denmark," Poulsen said. "It took me until the last year I was there to organise an Under-13s tournament between schools. It was the one year when the Chinese kids did not have exams and it was the small things like that which people don't think about but can make a real difference."

Around a quarter of Malaysians are of Chinese descent, and when there are barely any players in the league from that community then the whole system becomes weaker—for both clubs and the national team. In Singapore, where 75 percent of the population are Chinese, the contrast is more marked: only Gabriel Quak plays for the national team squad, so the country is really missing out.

The problem is that with fewer and fewer Chinese playing football, there are fewer role models for youngsters. At the turn of the century in the S-League, Lim Tong Hai, Steven Tan, Lee Man Hon and Goh Tat Chuan were all active. Now Chinese football players in the S-League are in danger of becoming extinct.

Jan Poulsen put some of it, at least, down to the Chinese penchant for education. "In Singapore, the family security was very important. The Chinese didn't allow their kids to play and that was a major problem." This has been a major problem for years. The story is a familiar one. In Chinese culture, parents traditionally want their children, their male children at least, to go in to a "good" career. Traditionally, Chinese (and not only in China but in other East Asian nations, too) parents rely on their boys to look after them financially in their dotage.

There could be footballing opportunities in other countries, but this option is rarely explored. Zainal Abidin Hassan had the chance to go to Saudi Arabia in the eighties. He turned it down.

"There was no encouragement to go. It was different then and more difficult. Of course, I regret. I think that if I make [sic] the first move then others will go. Today, still nobody has proven themselves overseas. We used to beat Korea and Japan and were better than them, but now they send players to Europe. Philippe Troussier told me that you need at least three brilliant players to lead the team and he said the more players that play abroad then the better it is for the national team."

In Singapore, Balestier Khalsa FC CEO S. Thavaneson agrees with

Zainal. "We have to get players playing abroad," he said when I asked his opinion in the bowels of the club's stadium, with cardboard boxes, pennants and posters around the office, giving off a real old-school football feeling. It is a place that can't have changed much since the eighties, and that is not a criticism but an appreciative observation. "The number of clubs in Singapore has fallen and now there are only six local clubs. Take out the foreign players from these clubs and how many local players do you have? If you are being generous you will say 25 a club."

A professional playing pool of around 150 is not much of a foundation from which to build, especially if you say that perhaps 20 are going to be too young and 20 too old. It makes sense, then, that with opportunities at home limited, players should travel. "They don't, though," noted Thavaneson. "They like to stay here. There are too many players in Singapore who don't want to better themselves. They are happy to come in and just play and then go home and do whatever with their friends. At this club, I don't want any player here who does not want to play for the national team. Whether they do or not is not the issue, they have to want to be as good as they can be."

Getting people from all races playing and getting as many overseas opportunities is just the start. Growing the player pool is vital and Penang president Zairil has a plan.

"The question is how you expand the pool of talent. If you do that you will find that there is talent everywhere. I am supporting and funding local junior leagues which are not organised by us. We had talks recently with local academies on how we can run a state-wide league for younger age groups and then expand the pool of talent and produce better and more Penang players for the future.

"You know what the best part of this is? These things don't cost so much money. I can [run] a league for a year with the salary I pay one player for one month in the Super League. There is so much you can do at that level with such little money, nobody is playing for money. The coaches are part-time, the boys just want to play, the parents will chip in and support them. It is a joy to watch football at that level. I enjoy watching them.

"Some of these academies have never been able to get their kids seen by the club as there was no bridge before; but now I am meeting these guys and attending tournaments and I see lots of potential. This is the way forward."

If technology presents a challenge in that when children do actually have some spare time, it is easy to spend it playing FIFA on a games console or messing about with an iPad or a smartphone, it can also help.

A high-speed rail link is being planned between Singapore, Kuala Lumpur and up into the north of Malaysia. There have been all kinds of such train stories over the years and there have been maps produced of Southeast Asia detailing all the proposed high speed rail lines pencilled in for the future. But this particular project will go ahead, and by the middle of the next decade Singapore and KL will be just a 90-minute train ride apart. Penang could be reached in just a few more hours.

This opens up opportunities for a genuine combined Malaysia-Singapore top division made up of S-League clubs and, hopefully, privatised Malaysian Super League teams. There is no need for shared cup competitions, but expanding the top tier with teams from both countries would be a boon. This would add excitement, money, commercial opportunities and playing opportunities for both countries.

Football has a unique power to bring people together and the rail link could contribute to this hugely. A look at football history shows that Malaysia and Singapore are at their strongest when they are at their closest. The shared history of the two countries is rich. The future could be, too.

ACKNOWLEDGEMENTS

There are a number of people I would like to thank. I am in debt to James Dampney and *FourFourTwo's* Southeast Asian office based in Singapore for allowing me to keep writing about this part of the world and the same goes for Jason Dasey at *ESPN Asia*. There seems to be something about JDs and Southeast Asian football.

Huge thanks to Lim Weixiang, *FourFourTwo's* talented photographer for providing the images.

Gerard Wong at *Today* was a real help with providing contacts, background and a deeper understanding of the Singapore scene and the same can be said of Haresh Deol, then editor of the *Malay Mail*.

Thank you to the people who agreed to give up their spare time and talk and much debt is owed to those who archived old newspapers from such titles as: *The Straits Times*, *The Singapore Free Press*, *The New Paper*, *New Nation*, *Malaya Tribune*, *Singapore Standard*, *Sunday Tribune*, *Malayan Saturday Post*.

Thanks to veteran reporter Joe Dorai whose reports for the *Straits Times* in the good old days really brought the past into life.

The book would not be possible with the fascinating history of football in the two countries and the people from Malaysia and Singapore—so friendly and welcoming.

She-reen Wong of Marshall Cavendish: we bonded in her office on a sunny October afternoon due to a shared connection to the Korean military, and she guided me through the process with patience and skill. Editor Mike Spilling helped to make many improvements and reduce at least some of the errors I made.

ABOUT THE AUTHOR

John Duerden hails from Blackburn in the United Kingdom and the London School of Economics graduate has been living in Asia since the end of the last century.

Married with two daughters, John has been covering Asian football for 20 years and contributes to *The New York Times*, *ESPN*, *BBC*, *FourFour Two*, *Associated Press*, *Today*, *World Soccer* and many more.

This is John's third book, following the best-selling *John Duerden Unlimited* published in South Korea in 2009 and *Wanderers, Rovers & Rangers*, published in the UK in 2017.